How to get into Marketing and PR

How to get into Marketing and PR

Annie Gurton

continuum
LONDON • NEW YORK

CONTINUUM

The Tower Building, 11 York Road, London SE1 7NX

370 Lexington Avenue, New York, NY 10017–6503

British Library Cataloguing-in-Publication Data

A catalogue record for this book is available from the British Library.

ISBN: 0-8264-6713-X (hardback) 0-8264-6714-8 (paperback)

Typeset by Hardlines Ltd

Printed and bound in Great Britain by Bookcraft (Bath) Ltd, Midsomer Norton, Somerset

Contents

Introduction

Marketing is the second oldest profession. Since the days when Adam tried to raise some interest in his apples and the process of presenting products and persuading customers was born, there has always been marketing. It was formalised as a professional career in the 1950s when universities and colleges started offering it as a course leading to a qualification, and since then it has steadily gained recognition and respect.

PR, or public relations, sometimes also press relations, is a subdivision of marketing. Marketing as an umbrella term includes advertising, market research, brand management and development, PR and promotion. While marketing is the strategic thinking and planning behind a sales campaign, PR is the process of creating a positive image in the minds of decision-makers and customers, so that they make the choice you want them to make. Both marketing and PR work together to capture new customers and keep them.

Marketing is a creative profession, but it also incorporates many other skills. Original thinking helps. For example, could you have dreamed up green ketchup or pyramid-shaped tea bags? They are both examples of marketing ideas, that marketing professionals created and then saw through product development, product launch and promotion to the customer.

What marketing is not – although often confused with it – is actually selling. True, marketing and selling are closely linked, but the act of closing a deal is the responsibility of the sales specialists, while the marketing professionals look at gaps in the market and how best to make the products appealing to increase the number of sales opportunities. Sometimes you see one person with a combined 'sales and marketing' job title, but the two tasks are different and require different skills.

What sort of person would choose marketing or PR as a career? Let's put it this way: it wouldn't suit the inhibited, inarticulate, shy or retiring. You need to be a psychologist and a salesman, intelligent and intuitive. A good marketing person has to be able to understand a market and know what customers will be looking for next. Good interpersonal and communication skills and the ability to get along with colleagues and clients using your intelligence and charm are essential requirements. A PR professional has to be able to party and schmooze and put a spin on a cliché to make you believe you've never heard it before. The trick for PRs is that they have to achieve these things without being patronising or sycophantic.

The good news is that job opportunities in marketing and PR are many and varied. And while many marketing professionals are high-profile flamboyant characters, there is also room for the quietly practical behind-the-scenes organiser. The marketing industry needs plodders as well as charmers and smarmers who can talk the hindleg off a donkey. Even the most upfront and confident PR person needs back-office workers who can arrange press events, and the nuts and bolts of marketing is the hard slog of painstaking and thorough market research.

Career progression can be fast, with someone finding themselves in a responsible, well-paid position within a year or so of starting as a junior. These days a degree and practical experience in marketing and PR are requirements for many jobs in top management and a place on the board. In fact, most boards these days have a marketing specialist representing the sales and PR activity, and many managing directors (MDs) or chief executive officers (CEOs) come from a marketing background.

What sort of courses should you be doing at school for a career in marketing and PR? Anything that requires communications and analysis skills such as English, history, geography, economics and any other arts course. Mathematics is also useful, because you'll have to set and manage budgets and will need to understand graphs and interpret statistics. Technology is increasingly important, particularly the use of the internet as a business and sales tool. You probably won't have to create a website, but you will need to understand about internet marketing. Some marketing professionals even started with a science background in technical development and progressed into product management before specialising in the marketing and promotion of those products. The single common factor is the ability to communicate ideas and enthusiasm.

PR and marketing require charm, tact and discretion. You'll find yourself working on new projects and products which will put your firm ahead of its competition. You'll hear secrets that you have to keep quiet, bad news you'll have to manage and good news that you'll have to spread. You have to win people over to your side, convince them that you are telling the truth. Consequently, loyalty is another attribute which is highly valued and sought after.

There is no average working environment for marketing or PR professionals. Some work for agencies with several clients in similar or complementary fields, while others work in-house for small, medium or large organisations. There are benefits and drawbacks to both agency and in-house working. Some marketing departments within large companies are bigger than some agencies, which can be one-man bands. Some large corporate organisations have in-house departments as well as using agencies, with the work divided up between them. Many marketing and PR professionals like to experience both, and many go on to start their own businesses or become partners in agencies. So you may find yourself working as part of a large team for several different clients, or just for one client. Alternatively you may be on your own, having to be a jack of all trades. In that case, you will have to think up the ideas and see them through, manage the brand development, organise the market research and plan your marketing campaigns all by yourself. But you'll probably start as a junior (also known as an account assistant or junior account manager) in an agency or an in-house department.

Most marketing and PR professionals specialise in one or two related vertical markets. For example, some work in the IT industry and know it inside out, understanding the technology and products, knowing the journalists and the big name vendors. Others focus on government issues or the public sector, while many move into fast-moving consumer goods (FMCG) which includes products like washing powder and foods. Then there is the financial sector, including insurance and investment firms and publishing, sport or fashion. Marketing professionals develop knowledge and expertise in the demands and trends of their chosen sector, as well as the general skills associated with marketing and PR. If you have a special interest or knowledge of a particular industry, such as IT or sport, then it makes sense to seek employment among firms or agencies working with companies and vendors in that sector. But it is a good idea to complete a general marketing or PR course at a university or college first, before focusing on your chosen speciality market.

When you are a PR professional you have to sell and promote without appearing to do so. If you push too hard the press campaign will flop and you'll waste a proportion of your budget. Worst of all, you'll lose credibility and that's the most important thing to a PR professional.

And if you work for an agency you'll find that you're caught between a rock and a hard place, with the client as the rock and the media as the hard place. They'll both expect to be the more important to you and you'll have to satisfy and please them both equally. They'll both blame you when it goes wrong. The answer is to treat them both as clients, and to do this you need great diplomacy and charm. If you can call up a journalist and not get a hostile brush-off, you'll know you're doing well – unfortunately, many journalists take great delight in tormenting and being rude to PR people.

A lot of people working in PR would actually prefer to be journalists but couldn't possibly live on the salary. Journalists – especially when they start – are paid very poorly (starting salaries of £6,000 a year are not unusual and even experienced editors often don't earn more than £25,000). So, many talented writers move into PR or marketing for the money. Salaries for marketing graduates with appropriate degrees usually start at £12,000–£15,000 but quickly rise to £20,000–£25,000. In-house marketing directors can easily earn £50,000 or more when they get to board level. If you run your own agency, once you are established, it is not unreasonable to expect to take over £100,000 out of the business every year.

Although degrees are preferred, there are also plenty of opportunities for those who have left school with practical skills or who have other talents which are appropriate for the job. It is quite common to find people with unconventional backgrounds working in marketing and PR roles. And once in the business, it is relatively easy to get promoted on the basis of your performance, skills and track record rather than your formal qualifications.

Although contact with journalists and clients is an important part of your job, much of your time will be spent working on planning and reports. You will be involved in preparing and delivering presentations and there is a lot of budget-setting, negotiating and defining of objectives, analysis of research and forecasting and writing reviews of campaign performance and feedback and recommendations on future activities.

You have to understand your target market and know the channels of communication, which these days includes the internet as well as traditional routes like print media, television, radio and video, plus sponsorship and other promotional activity. In marketing in particular, you have to know the jargon. What is the marketing mix, for example, and what is the Boston Matrix? What is profiling and segmentation, what is a focus group, and how does an audit work? What is brand extension? How do you devise a marketing campaign to meet the needs of the aspirational group? What is a SWOT analysis? You'll learn the answers to all these on your marketing course at college or university.

Marketing is full of buzzwords, three-letter acronyms (TLAs) and theories. You will have to know the nuts and bolts of marketing theory – in this book we give you the main principles and terms which you have to know to get by. There are also some fairly important people you should know about. For example, who is Charles Handy and what does he say that's important to marketers? Who is Abraham Maslow and why is his hierarchy of needs so important? Then there are Alfred P. Sloan, Peter Drucker and Theodore Levitt – you need to know what these people said if you are to have credibility.

Marketing is a crucial activity on which rests the success or failure of any company, product or service. Marketing starts long before the products are made and continues long after the products have been sold. You help shape people's images and impressions – every marketing and PR professional has to understand and practise a bit of economics, psychology and sociology. It's fun, exciting and challenging.

What more could anyone want in a career?

Accountant

Money: Not a lot before qualification and often starting at £15,000 once qualified. But the rates improve rapidly and once you have a proven track record in the marketing industry and can claim to be an industry specialist, you can earn £30,000–£35,000. The finance director will be on £50,000 at least, and probably nearer £100,000.

Hours: Conventional, at least compared with some other marketing jobs. Usually 9–5, Monday–Friday, with overtime rarely required unless you become involved in a client pitch or a campaign. There is little need to socialise with clients or creative types, although if you want there is nothing to stop you joining the creative teams down the pub after work. The amount of after-work socialising you do is up to you, rather than being obligatory.

Health risk: Low. You are mainly sitting in an office working at computer screens. You'll probably have to schedule sports and fitness activities into your routine because they are not there naturally, unless you count running for a bus or walking up a few flights of stairs.

Pressure rating: Depends on your level of seniority, but the more money you earn the greater your responsibility and therefore the greater pressure you'll be under.

Glamour rating: Low. Accountancy never has a high glamour profile, but a creative individual can turn a mundane accounting job into a creative and more interesting one by becoming more involved in the marketing process.

Travel rating: Low. You are unlikely to get on press jollies or go to glamorous foreign locations on research assignments, and will probably be the last one to be invited to lunch with clients or creative professionals. But it does happen.

Every marketing agency needs either an in-house or external accountant to manage its financial affairs. In-house marketing departments find that they have to work closely with the firm's accountants to justify their existence and make sure that they are effective. A good accountant can do far more than balance the books, however.

If you are good with figures and have a logical, methodical mind, someone might suggest that you become an accountant and you might groan and discount the idea immediately. Accounting is a boring profession, surely! But accountants in marketing and PR firms can share in the glamour and excitement of creating and developing ideas and seeing them through to a successful conclusion.

Raj Patel, financial director of a top marketing agency, says that accountants are crucial. 'They help set budgets and work out the costs of managing a campaign, and are involved in ensuring that products under development are not going to cost too much to be viable. They make sure that the marketing projects make money and everyone involved can get paid and the product or service being promoted is cost-effective and profitable.'

Raj started his career by studying accountancy at university, mainly because his father wanted him to. 'I thought it would be boring, but by working in marketing it is a lot more exciting than I expected,' he says. Marketing accountants start with the same accountancy training as those in any other field. This involves at least three years full-time at college or university or working for an accountancy firm and attending a college on day-release, spreading the examinations over more time. There are several levels of qualification, starting with a basic accreditation confirming that you can manage the accounting software and produce basic accounts, but you'll need to be fully qualified to get the best jobs within marketing firms or with an external accountancy practice that specialises in marketing businesses. Full qualification also involves knowing the law relating to accounting and business management and the legal and statutory obligations on marketing firms.

Raj says, 'After following the conventional route for accountants and passing the exams, you can start to specialise.' He explains that another route is to start with a marketing agency as a junior in the accounts department, ensuring that the bills get paid and invoices are dealt with. This helps you learn how to work with figures and determines whether you would make a good accountant. 'The accounts department often also has to deal with the firm's payroll and work with freelance subcontractors who work with the agency, such as video producers, copywriters or **market research** samplers, so you can get a broad range of expertise from one junior job. However, you need to be fully qualified if you want to be any more than an assistant in the accounts department.'

As you progress, and after you qualify, you can eventually rise to finance director, often the most senior accounting role in the agency. At this level you are seriously involved in all aspects of the marketing agency, from pitching for new business to creating new campaigns, managing old products and developing existing products into new areas to extend their lifespan, as well as ensuring that the firm remains profitable.

How to get into Marketing and PR

The accountant is often relied upon to keep the creative types' feet on the ground. Raj says, 'The account executives might decide that a boring old bit of plastic gizmo which used to sell like hot cakes would take off again if only it could be made fluorescent. They start talking about the advertising jingle, the catchline, the video and the new markets and names of stars they could use to promote the product. The accountant has to point out that fluorescent paint is very expensive and will put up the **price** of each gizmo by 500 per cent and, anyway, there is another fluorescent gizmo on the market which probably has a patent on it. You point out that the costs of altering the production line will be prohibitive. You also mention that working with fluorescent paint is included in the latest health and safety rulings and workers have to have an extra four weeks' holiday and regular health checks to make sure they are not becoming ill. And are the creatives sure that customers will really want a fluorescent gizmo?' Yet Raj adds that becoming involved in these sorts of decision on creative issues is what makes working in the world of marketing fun for someone with an accounting background.

Raj says that accountants with experience in the marketing industry will be able to spot whether budgeted items have been under- or over-costed. 'For example, the account manager might have estimated that the cost of running an advertising campaign on digital radio is £20,000 a year, but the accountant will know that it is possible to get very good coverage through some of the new digital radio agencies for under £10,000 a year. The accountant will query it and either reduce the cost in the budget or let it stay knowing that the final costs will probably be less than the budgeted figure. This will give the firm either an area where they can come in under budget, or a cushion against which an unexpectedly high cost elsewhere can be absorbed. The accountant should also be the one to spot that there has been no allocation in the budget for press cuttings, for which an agency needs in order to be paid.'

Unlike many marketing and PR professionals, the accountant will probably have to wear a suit. Raj says, 'Even though being an accountant in the world of marketing is more creative than being an accountant in many other industries, it is still once of the more conventional jobs with traditional expectations. Although many firms and departments will allow accountants to wear "smart but casual" clothes when they are going to be in the office all day, if they are meeting clients then a suit will be expected, while the creative types can probably get away with more relaxed garb.' Accountants, along with lawyers, are expected to be the respectable face of a business and have to dress accordingly.

You often have to work as part of a team and the ability to get along with all sorts, and be able to talk to clients, is essential. Unlike many other jobs in marketing, that of the accountant is based on clear rules and precedents, so in many ways it is easier to learn. But if you are to advance on the career ladder, you'll also need plenty of 'soft' interpersonal skills, like the ability to make a presentation and to run staff appraisals. Accountants are frequently expected to keep an eye on the financial and management press and report to the product development directors if they spot new market opportunities or believe that a current market does not have a long lifespan. They are sometimes the antennae of the marketing team, looking for financial and customer buying trends, making sure that new markets are explored and developed if appropriate. They should be able to spot international opportunities and help plan the overall strategy of the firm.

In short, once accountants become established in the world of marketing and start moving up the career ladder, they find that their responsibilities cover far more than just ensuring that the accounts are done on time and accurately, and returns are made to Companies House. They'll be involved in all aspects of the business and all stages of the campaign life cycle.

Raj says, 'Being an accountant involves a precise and demanding training which, for the right mind that likes order and systems, is not at all boring. And for accountants that choose to specialise in the marketing industry, there is plenty of excitement and fun. It is also an essential part of the marketing role, and greatly valued (although not always appreciated) by other marketing and PR professionals.'

Skills you'll need

- A head for figures. As well as a basic understanding of the principles of double-entry bookkeeping, you'll have to understand statistics and reports, surveys and budgets.
- Good people skills which enable you to get along with creative types who have no time for figures, even though they are essential.
- You'll have to learn the principles of marketing and know the classic marketing theories.
- An intelligent, analytical mind combined with eloquence allows a career in accountancy to be combined with a career in marketing and will enable you to get the best of both worlds.

- Start with basic accounting training or a job in the accounts department of a marketing firm and then move on to learn about the marketing industry later.
- Subscribe to magazines for accountancy professionals, like *Accounting* and *Accountancy Age* and read the news and features carefully. Also subscribe to *Marketing* and *Marketing Week*, to gain familiarity with terms and current campaigns.
- Learn an accounting software package. Once you've mastered that, learn a reporting package and how to extrapolate meaningful business and marketing decisions from accounts.

Glossary

- **Market research**
  The systematic gathering, recording and analysis of information, views, opinions and facts which affect decisions on sales, marketing and PR.
- **Price**
  The value of a product or service which is deemed fair by both vendor and customer.

Advertising account executive or manager

Money: You might have to start at around £15,000 but this could rise to £20,000 or £25,000 within a year. Perks might include gym membership or private healthcare. Depending on the product, you might get lots of samples.

Hours: As with most creative jobs, account managers often work slightly later days than, say, accountants. So 10–6 would be normal.

Health risk: Low. The working environment should be safe – there's not much that can attack you in an office apart from the colds and flu doing the rounds. You are more likely to suffer from hangovers caused by your enthusiastic efforts to network and impress the account director and the rest of the team.

Pressure rating: Medium. Although you won't have ultimate responsibility you will be expected to make sure that everything happens smoothly. You will get the blame for any screw-ups, so the pressure will be on.

Glamour rating: Could be good. Depending on the client and the market sector, it could be excellent. Contrariwise, handling the advertising for a toothpaste isn't going to impress many people.

Travel rating: Again, varies according to the client and the market. But if there is any opportunity to travel the chances are that the account director will take it.

In-house marketing departments don't have account executives or account managers, as they have just one client. This job title is only relevant in advertising and marketing agencies and consultancies which have many clients, each called an account. The account executive or account manager (the terms vary from agency to agency – sometimes they are called client managers) reports to the account director and is responsible for the day-to-day running of the clients' business. In some agencies, the lowest rung on the ladder is the account executive and the account manager is senior. In some it is the other way around.

Advertising is another subdivision of marketing, like PR, and requires special skills, as well as general marketing knowledge.

Advertising is the mass communication part of promotion, and promotion is one of the essential **4 Ps** of marketing.

Sheena Smith has specialised in advertising since she did a marketing degree at the University of London and is now an account director with a medium-sized agency which specialises in women's fashion and cosmetics. She says, 'The objective of advertising is to reach as wide an audience as possible, to raise their awareness of the product or service being promoted and to persuade them to buy it.'

According to Sheena, 'Advertising can be oriented towards delivering information, for example to acquaint customers with new store hours or a new website or to remind and persuade them to choose the store, service or product.' She believes that advertising aims include to increase **brand** recognition and improve the brand image, so the advertising must be closely linked with the profile of the customer for that brand. 'Products for young people, for example, require a different type of advertisement to those targeted at businesses or senior citizens,' she says. 'It's obvious really, but in fact there is a lot of science and research behind all the decisions and strategies that we initiate.'

Account executive could be your first job in marketing. Many agencies have a post called junior advertising account executive or junior account manager. 'That's how I started after university,' says Sheena. 'Some account managers have been in the job for three or four years – if you've been doing it for more than five you can probably assume that you are never going to be promoted to account director.'

The account executive or manager, particularly at junior level, will be the team dogsbody. You'll have to make sure that everything is happening to schedule and ensure that project management deadlines are met so that no aspect of the campaign gets behind. You'll need to liaise with production staff to ensure that the advertising and promotional materials are all produced on time and are accurate. A typo on a hoarding, for example, would not only create huge problems with the client but might produce a negative reaction, the opposite of what was intended. T-shirts with the wrong slogan or an old logo might become collectors' items – but you'd get the sack.

The account executive is often assigned to just a few accounts, while the account director may be in charge of a larger group of accounts, delegating tasks to the executives. Sometimes the account executive only works on one account, if it is a big one. Some accounts will have two or three executives working on them exclusively, in which case there will be a hierarchy of seniority among the account managers.

Sheena says, 'The account managers don't have a lot of responsibility except to carry out a range of administrative tasks efficiently and reliably. But, as you progress, these responsibilities will increase and you will be judged on how effectively you carry these out. You will attend some client meetings along with the account director and will work fairly closely with some client staff. You'll also work with others in the creative team, especially freelancers and independents.'

As a new account executive, your first task is to become fully familiar with the client's products and undertake your own research on the market and its competitors. You'll have to take part in the creative brainstorming sessions and if you make some interesting contributions you'll be noticed by the account director. You won't be expected to be highly creative – the account executive role is an action job, making sure that everything happens when it should.

Sheena says, 'As the junior you may get roped in to be part of the field testing, **sampling** or being a "mystery shopper" to check the success and impact of a campaign. You might also expect to do some "vox pops" or street questionnaires, so you must have enough self-confidence to walk up to complete strangers and ask them their views!'

After client meetings it is often left to the account manager to produce a report for the others on the team and for the client. So you'll need to talk notes during the meetings and be able to transcribe them afterwards.

'As you progress you'll develop your own database of freelancers and independents – this little black book will develop and grow throughout your career and will differentiate you from other executives looking for promotion. So start one on your first day, keep it continuously updated and look after it carefully,' says Sheena.

As a fairly junior member of the team you'll be expected to be conscientious and smart. The clothes you choose to wear will be taken as an indication of your seriousness, so don't be too casual. Originality can fast-track you to director level or it can ensure that you get fired, so be careful about being too outrageous. Sheena says, 'Sometimes it's hard to keep your thoughts in check, but it is best to strike a balance between being noticed for hard, conscientious work and being a pain in the neck to your work colleagues. You have to get it right.'

Skills you'll need

- You'll have to be able to observe, watch and learn and be prepared to work on your own initiative. You can't always

How to get into Marketing and PR

wait to be told what to do, but have to know when you need authority to take a decision. For example, the account manager will be expected to spot a problem before it happens, such as a clash of advertisement bookings, but to tell the account director, not the client.

■ You must be able to be discreet – you'll hear lots of confidential information which could cause great trouble if your clients' competitors heard about it.

■ You'll need a good eye for detail – someone else will be taking care of the bigger picture.

■ You'll also need to know how to deal with journalists – some see account managers as a potential weak link in the chain and may target you to find out more about a campaign.

■ Of course you'll be expected to have basic familiarity with a word processor and e-mail. You'll probably learn how to download image files and transfer them around the team; later, you'll learn how to use a spreadsheet.

Tips

■ This is the first or second rung on your marketing or advertising career ladder and if you show promise you can get onto the fast track.

■ In meetings with clients you won't be expected to say anything, although interesting and eloquent contributions will probably be welcomed. But it's better to be quiet than to say the wrong things.

■ Many advertising agencies use temporary staff for a variety of jobs through the lifetime of a campaign – being used as a temp can be a back-door way into an agency.

Glossary

■ **Brand**
A name, logo, term, design or 'atmosphere' that uniquely identifies a product or service.

■ **4 Ps**
A specific combination of marketing elements is used to achieve an organisation or individual's objectives and satisfy the target market, usually having four major variables: product, promotion, price and place (location).

■ **Sampling**
Analysis of a selected small group of customers.

Advertising copywriter

Money:	Depends a lot on your skills and experience and the fame of the campaigns and slogans you have devised and worked on. Probably starting at around £16,000 but reaching £45,000 for top-notch writers.
Hours:	There will be plenty of meetings during conventional office hours, but a lot of creative inspiration comes at the oddest times of the day – even in the bath!
Health risk:	Minimal.
Pressure rating:	Medium. There are always deadlines and difficult clients to deal with, so the ability to work under pressure is essential.
Glamour rating:	Medium, depending on the clients you work with.
Travel rating:	Low. You may get the occasional trip to a client meeting but most of your work will be done at your desk.

All the words on all advertisements and all marketing material have to be written and this requires real writing talent. It is not about writing a novel or bestselling story, but about having a way with words and the ability to catch the customers' eye.

Maria Boxer has always shown an aptitude for writing and when she studied literature at university it was with a career as a novelist in mind. 'I saw myself getting one of those enormous publishers' advances that you read about,' she says, 'but it was not to be.' The pressure of living in the real world and the need to earn a living took her to a PR agency, where she wrote press releases, but she says she hated that because of the involvement of clients. 'They would make changes which I knew were grammatically wrong, but I had to use them.' Eventually she found she had a talent for writing snappy headlines and took this to an advertising agency, where she has now been for three years.

Maria explains, 'I think it was Churchill who said that he didn't have time to write a two-page letter but he'd write a five-page one instead. It is much harder to writer short, sweet, succinct **messages** and slogans than long reports and some people have the skill and others don't.' She says that she does crosswords, which she believes helps develop the art. 'I love words,' she says, 'and although I still dream about being a novelist and I'm working on a book in my spare time at the moment, I also enjoy working as an advertising copywriter.'

The agency that Maria works for specialises in fashion and women's products, like clothes and cosmetics, so she writes for several clients on campaigns that might compete. 'That's odd sometimes, seeing competing adverts and I've written the words for both of them, but it doesn't happen very often,' she says.

Maria is involved right from the initial meetings with clients, after the contract with them has been signed. She has to interpret the client's often vague ideas of what the brand should represent and what the brand values should be and come up with slogans and copy which reinforce and project what they want to say. 'Sometimes it is a real challenge to get to the heart of what the client really wants and I always have to do at least six or seven different ideas.'

She works with the creative team to come up with words which fit best with the illustration they have devised. 'Sometimes they just want one or two short, snappy words, other times I have to write a complete paragraph or two explaining the product further.'

Maria also has to write the words that go on packaging and collateral sales material, and point-of-sale promotional material. 'The range of writing for one campaign is surprisingly big,' she says. 'I have to write the advert itself and then variations for different media like TV or magazines. Then I have to write at least ten or fifteen other documents, often taking the slogan or message that the client has chosen and re-presenting it in different ways.'

Copywriting was once a 'hidden' skill in the back room of many agencies, but these days the copywriters are often the stars. Maria says, 'There is a lot of kudos to be had for the copywriter who devises particular advertising campaigns that have passed into the lingua franca. For example, one of my heroines is Fay Weldon, the writer, and she was responsible for the 'Go to Work on an Egg' catchphrase which was very popular in the seventies. In fact, she has gone from being a copywriter to being a very successful author and that's the career path I'd like to follow.'

Maria is also studying Spanish because she wants to work abroad – a bilingual ability would open many doors, she says. 'I would like to work in the USA as well as Europe, and Spanish is one of the most widely-spoken languages in the world. To be able to speak it well enough to write in colloquial Spanish is a big challenge, but I think I can do it if I study hard.'

- Your English, obviously, needs to be very hot. You must have an excellent grounding in grammar and literature and the ability to devise catchphrases and snappy slogans.
- You need to be a 'people person' because there will be plenty of dealing with clients and other marketing professionals. You have to be diplomatic to be able to deal with clients and skillful at working with other creative people such as the art and design teams. You have to work with the production people, too, to talk about deadlines and to make sure that the words you write fit the pages and spaces available.

Tips

- You can start writing your own slogans any time, but a good way to get your brain working is by doing both cryptic and simple crosswords. Maria says, 'Crosswords are the best way to improve your word skills and your ability to think of alternative words or words which convey impressions.'

Glossary

- **Message**
  A combination of words, symbols and images which imparts a required impression to the target market.

Advertising director

Money: Pretty good, but you'll probably have been in advertising for at least five years before you make director. Directors start on around £30,000 and can reach £70,000 or £80,000. Perks might include bonuses, private healthcare and gym membership. There will probably be a pension scheme.

Hours: The higher you get up the career ladder, the more demands are going to be made on you. By the time you get to be director you'll be expected to work whatever hours are required. But if you are a good director you'll be able to delegate and manage, getting other people to cover overtime while you tell them what to do.

Health risk: Low in terms of physical risk – there's not much chance of breaking a leg in the office. Medium in terms of sedentary working style – you'll need to schedule in exercise breaks to make sure you keep fit. High risk, though, from the consequences of stress and meals which are either unhealthy (over-the-top expense account lunches) or rushed sandwiches.

Pressure rating: High. Stress levels will increase the more senior you become and the more campaigns you manage. Campaigns also have a life cycle and the further a campaign develops the higher the stress level starts to rise. As director, you'll be expected to carry the can.

Glamour rating: High. With luck you can take all the credit for a successful campaign and the client will nominate you for an industry award.

Travel rating: Depends on the industry and clients you are working with, but can be excellent. Advertising directors often have to accompany the creative team when they film or photograph the images and that might require a trip to a distant glamorous location. You might also have to travel to industry conferences (both advertising industry conferences and those of the markets you specialise in), to make sure that you remain at the forefront.

This is the big cheese, the person responsible for the overall control and management of an advertising campaign. If the client has a grouse, the buck stops with the account director. You'll be responsible for keeping the client happy and that means interpreting their instructions, reading between the lines about their requirements, and making sure that they think they get what they want.

Andrea Smith has worked for many years as a PR and advertising director and says that by the time you get to the account director level you should have quite a bit of experience of running campaigns and dealing with clients. 'This is a highly responsible senior job,' she says. 'It will be your job to develop an advertising plan and the more of these you do the easier they become.'

Starting as an account manager or executive is the best route to becoming a director, Andrea says. 'You pick up lots of hints and tips as time goes on and you learn a little from each campaign and carry it forward to future ones.'

Account directors have to be able to manage several internal and freelance teams of creative and practical types and make sure that different people are working on different aspects at the right time. 'The account director has to understand project management, as well as knowing the business of advertising,' Andrea adds.

You'll also have to ensure that there is a steady revenue stream from various clients. As an agency director, you'll have a portfolio of clients of different sizes and budgets. Andrea explains, 'It will be up to you to ensure that their money is spent wisely and they get to see good results from the campaigns you initiate and run. You'll have to develop new business revenues for the agency from current and prospective clients. You'll have to develop, implement and manage internal company initiatives for the benefit of the agency as a whole.'

The director will set out the objectives of the campaign, in conjunction with the client. In meetings with the client, it is usually the account director who chairs the session but he or she will have to defer to the client's position – they pay the salaries. Products go through a life cycle and you have to understand how campaigns need to change to match the different stages.

According to Andrea, 'The campaign objectives might be to get a slogan imprinted on the minds of the customers or to introduce a new catchphrase which will be used in all sorts of marketing material for the next year. With these in place the director then has to choose the team, making sure that all jobs and functions are covered. It's no good getting into a campaign and then realising that there is no one with any expertise in selecting the media that the campaign will run in. At this stage it may be decided that it is necessary to bring in outside specialists, such as photographers, video directors or web developers.

'Next step is to set the budget and to do this you'll have to work with the accountant and the client. Set a budget that's too low and you'll have trouble keeping within it and delivering quality. If it's too high the client will complain and possibly even move to another, cheaper agency. The budget will include the agency's fees as well as all the media and running costs, plus a contingency element for unexpected expenses. Experience will enable the director to guess a budget and then, when they come to confirm it later using a spreadsheet on a computer, they'll find that they are almost spot-on.'

After that, the director will sit down with his creative team and brainstorm, coming up with ideas for catchphrases, themes, images and so forth. This is when the look and feel of the campaign starts to take shape. With the copywriter and a designer, rough images are produced and catchlines developed. A selection of these is then whittled down to a few and either a decision is taken then or the shortlist is referred to the client for a decision. The client has the final word, but the advice of the agency is usually taken into account.

Then a detailed media plan is developed with the media buyer, combining all the elements such as billboard, radio, television, cinema, newspapers, magazines and so forth, keeping within the budget.

After that the advertisements are created while the media buyer uses high-level negotiating skills to get the best slots at the best rates.'Once the campaign is finished the director will be responsible for evaluating the success or failure, using the original objectives and some market research to get measurable facts,' says Andrea.'The director will then have a final meeting with the client, a post mortem at which the campaign is dissected and criticised, so that everyone can learn how it can be improved next time.'

The account director is often in charge of a large cluster of accounts, delegating tasks to the executives or account managers, who each have a few accounts to deal with or even just one.

Andrea says, 'After a campaign, you'll need to be thinking how you can keep the client for another campaign in the near future. Clients sometimes think it's a good idea to keep changing agencies – you must convince them that loyalty and stability are in their best interest.'

Skills you'll need

- The account director will have to manage a team of in-house and third-party people, many of them temperamental, creative types. They also have to take primary responsibility for dealing with the client. All this requires top interpersonal and management skills, to motivate and energise the team, to inspire them to create something original and to make sure the campaign runs properly.
- You'll have to be able to see the big picture while others take care of the details. But you must be able to spot a detail that isn't right – after all, you're going to have ultimate responsibility.
- You have to be able to work within a budget – and you might have to tell a creative person that their good idea can't

be used because it's too expensive. This is a combined creative and management job which requires good skills in both areas.

- You'll also have to manage more than one team at once, so the ability to think about lots of jobs and deadlines simultaneously will be useful.
- You'll have to be well organised and able to make sure those in the team are well organised too – not always easy when the team includes lots of creative types.

Tips

- You need all-round talents so cultivate close working relationships with both creative and management people, even if you think that your strengths lie in one area or the other.
- You need to get along with all sorts of people – if your career aim is to become a director, remember that the people you meet on the way up are going to be very important to you.
- Watch, look and learn from the way other directors work. When you are a junior, observe the way your director manages people and clients and runs the campaign – see what you could do better, but keep your thoughts to yourself until you are appointed director!
- Try to experience all the jobs that you'll be delegating and managing. People have far more respect and take instructions better when the director is someone who knows what they are talking about.
- Many agencies recruit graduates looking for first-time jobs and train them internally. You could precipitate the process by approaching an agency that you'd like to work for and asking them about their graduate recruitment programmes – they like people who aren't slow to come forward and being proactive will probably give you an advantage. Remember that jobs in advertising are in high demand.
- You could also approach the best agencies and ask for work experience – sometimes they are looking for juniors just for the duration of a campaign and it can be your chance to demonstrate what you can do. Some agencies routinely recruit temporary workers for field sampling and to be 'mystery shoppers'– again, this can be a back-door way into an agency.

Advertising layout designer

See *Art director*. Designing the layout of advertisements is one of the jobs that the art director and his team are responsible for.

Advertising media buyer

See *Media buyer*.

Advertising production manager

See **Production manager**, whose job will include managing the production of advertisements, along with other print.

Art director

Money: As a junior in a design studio you might have to start at £10,000 but as you demonstrate your originality and creativity that will rise to £20,000–£30,000 depending on experience and reputation. Eventually you might become a freelancer working for lots of clients on individual projects or a specialist in advertising or package or website design and your income could top £80,000.

Hours: Unconventional. If you prefer to work early mornings or late at night, you usually can, although when you start you might have to work more conventional office hours in a design studio. Creative work is rarely limited to 9–5 and most employers recognise this.

Health risk: Provided you don't suck your pens or sniff the adhesive or fixative spray, there is not a lot of risk to creative work.

Pressure rating: Medium to high. This can be a problem, as many creative types are unable to cope with the pressure of deadlines or working with clients. But to work successfully in an advertising or PR department or agency, the creative person has to be able to marry their artistic temperament with business common sense and interpersonal skills.

Glamour rating: Medium to high, depending on the client or project that you are working on or responsible for. Many art directors are famous (or infamous) for the way they challenge convention and set themselves apart from the crowd.

Travel rating: Low to medium. There are sometimes opportunities to travel, either locally or internationally, perhaps to meet clients or for location work, but generally most art and design people are tied to their studios.

When it comes to visual creative talent, this is the department where it all happens. You'll know the creative team because they dress distinctively and have quirky visual mannerisms, like large coloured glasses, bow ties or long hair when everyone else is wearing it short or vice versa. They like to stand out and shout 'I am an arty type' by being different from the crowd. The worst thing a creative designer can do is wear a plain suit – unless everyone else is dressing down, in which case they will want to wear a suit to stand out.

Pauline Carpenter is now a freelance designer but has held many jobs within agencies after starting as a junior in an in-house marketing department with an international computer software firm. She started as the junior in the firm at 19 after doing an HND at college. 'I specialised in graphics design,' she says, 'and wanted to get to work as soon as possible.'

She says she loves the work for the variety and creative opportunities. 'Of course I have to work to a brief, but I also have plenty of scope to be creative and innovative. That's what the clients want – things that look individual and unique.'

Everyone in the creative team has to work with the brand and product managers and the marketing manager on all sorts of design projects. Pauline says, 'One day you'll find yourself creating new logos and packages for products. Sometimes you will have to refresh old designs, sometimes create distinctive new designs for new brands.'

Many designers specialise, either within agencies or marketing departments or as freelancers. Pauline's speciality is advertising and creative visuals and storyboards for TV adverts. 'I have to work with a lot of TV creative people, which I enjoy very much although they are a mad bunch,' she says.

You might specialise in packaging, creating visual rough designs and then final images for the manager in charge of the client or reporting direct to the marketing manager. Pauline says, 'Whatever you do, you'll have to interpret often vague descriptions of a marketing or brand manager's idea into a design on computer or paper. Or you might specialise in promotion design, developing new wrappers and special effect boxes for products so that they are distinctive and appeal to customers' **brand loyalty** when they are selecting what to buy.' Design can be very satisfying, particularly if you are responsible for a successful but simple design that says a lot, such as the Nike tick or the McDonald's M.

Pauline says, 'Designs might be created by traditional methods like paper, pencil and ink but new technologies are widely used. You won't just have to know how to interpret a visual into a computer version, you'll also know how to integrate multimedia techniques and use different media to develop an image to make it unique.'

You won't necessarily have a completely free hand when designing visuals. Every commission will come with a list of constraints, such as that it must be a certain colour. Pauline says, 'Sometimes, a logo that you design must be usable on a lot of different items and in a lot of different ways, such as letterheading, neon advertising and sponsorship as well as just the package of the product. When designing packaging, for example, you might have to specify the material that is used, such as Styrofoam, cellophane, plastic or cardboard and you have to understand the financial and functional differences, benefits and disadvantages of each.'

You won't be responsible for the actual words that are used in adverts or on packages – that will be up to the copywriters and product managers. Your responsibility will be purely to design the layout and images so that they appeal to the customers and stay in their memory. The more instantly recognisable the image, the more successful you will be seen to be. Your job is to differentiate through the visual image all advertising, packaging and promotional material so that customers immediately recognise it and want the product.

There are fashions in design as in everything else and, currently, certain bright colours are in vogue, although there is always a place for black and white. Shapes are currently plain and smoothly curved, although there is always a place for fussy and traditional 'retro' designs.

Once you've designed a new image you'll have to check with the lawyers that it doesn't conflict with a legally registered logo or image, and with the brand manager that it portrays the image they want.

You'll have to know about film and video and the internet, as well as traditional pen and paper and computer-based design methods. And although it doesn't appear to use visuals, you might also have to think about how your designs can be linked to radio broadcasts and advertising and how the image can be conveyed without actually being seen.

You'll have to think about the long-term use of your designs and images as well as the immediate benefits and costs; take environmental and safety considerations into account; and be aware of the messages that the brand manager wants the advertising and promotional material to promote and underpin.

Skills you'll need

- An arts and graphics background is essential and you'll probably have shown talent in this direction from an early age. You'll like drawing and will have good draughtsmanship, even if you are not necessarily able to capture an image.
- You'll have to know your art history and be able to make connections between what people want today and traditional art and design.
- The ability to interpret and translate what people say into a visual that matches the idea they have in their mind.
- **IT** skills will be important, as well as traditional design and drafting skills. You'll have to be able to use the latest design software packages, as well as web design software to design websites.

- An original, creative mind is essential. You can learn a lot from other designers but you'll need to be able to submit images that are original and not derivative.

Tips

- Keep drawing! All artistic professionals are natural designers and doodlers and demonstrate their flair from an early age.
- Hang on to all the work you produce – when you look back at your early work in years to come you might find inspiration.

Glossary

- **Brand loyalty**
  The consistent preference towards repurchasing a particular brand to the exclusion of any other. The consumer feels comfortable and is attempting to remove risk, time and thought.
- **IT**
  Information technology.

Brand manager

Money: Starting at around £15,000 but reaching £30,000 or more as you gain experience. Many marketing directors have been brand managers in the past, so it is a good career stepping stone.

Hours: Regular, often 10–6 with occasional overtime.

Health risk: Minimal. This is mainly a deskbound and management job, with few risks apart from the danger of tripping over a computer cable.

Pressure rating: Medium. As you get more experience and responsibility, your decisions and judgments can have crucial effects on the survival and development of a brand. If you get it wrong, the brand might have to be dropped with knock-on effects through the whole company, from factory to distribution and other management departments. So you must get the branding right.

Glamour rating: Depends who you work for and the brand image you achieve. Some brands have such a bad profile that it rubs off on those associated with it. If you are responsible for a great brand, however, that reflects on you personally too.

Travel rating: Low. Unless you work for a global brand and have to visit company offices in other cities, apart from travel to meetings with agencies there won't be much travel for you.

Arguably the most widely known brands on the planet are McDonald's, Coke and Nike – all aimed mainly at the youth market. Wherever you go in the world, you are unlikely to be far from a logo or image which is instantly recognisable and creates an immediate link with certain emotions. As brand manager, your job will be to develop and spread positive connotations of the image, so that if a customer sees your company or product logo, they get a good feeling and want to buy the product.

The brand manager's job is to make better use of existing brand names as well as deepening the appeal of currently successful brands. This depends on a combination of packaging, promotion and strategy. The name, design, symbol or logo or any other feature that identifies the goods or services not only differentiates your product from others, but is also associated with certain emotions and creates a feeling of safety and loyalty. The earliest brands originated in the Middle Ages when the craft and merchant guilds required each producer to mark goods so that output could be restricted and quality maintained. The marks served as standards and many of the goods on sale today are based on brands established in the nineteenth century, for example Pears Soap, Quaker Oats, Vaseline and Dunlop.

Steve Phillips is an in-house brand manager with a large household products manufacturer. He says that brands are changing so fast these days because of the new media technologies. 'Just look at what the internet has done to brands in the music, books, banking and travel sectors. Old brands have to be reinvented and new brands have to evolve fast with credibility and be able to stand on their own next to the old ones in a matter or weeks, if not days.'

The greatest level of consumer appeal and profits go to the brands which are honestly and rigorously dedicated to strong image development. Steve says that the brand manager is looking at how current brands can be developed and extended. The cost of launching a new product under an existing brand is far less than having to invest in new packaging, logo development, product naming, advertising and other promotional costs. 'So not only do you get new flavours under one brand of sweets, for example, but you will also get a sweet brand appearing on other food products like jam and fizzy drinks or ice cream. Household names which achieve popularity pop up in all sections of the supermarket, some more successfully than others. Brand management used to be about doing a big launch and then putting a steady hand on the tiller. Now, brands need continual reinvention to stay alive. This demands proactive marketing and it needs agencies and consultancies that are not precious about changing their strategies and modes of thinking.' Brand marketers have to act more creatively than they used to, says Steve. 'It's all about keeping the brand fresh.'

You are a consumer, so you know which brand images make you feel confident, reassured and safe, and which are less successful. Steve says that sometimes the connection is achieved through association with a celebrity or star who is used in the advertising – through their voice and face the brand profile is reinforced and strengthened. 'These connections are called "branding" and help persuade people to choose one product over a competitor,' he says. Ultimately, a successful brand will virtually sell itself and products developed under a **brand-extension** strategy will have an immediate advantage in the market.

There are certain brands which have been developed specifically for the internet, like egg and amazon.com, but the fundamentals of electronic brand management are not much different from those of conventional brand management. The objective is still to create loyalty through trust.

As brand manager, you have a budget to manage and develop the brand, some of which will go to designers and the rest to market researchers. You'll also work with the marketing director or manager to devise a strategy for the continuing development of existing brands and the launch of new products and brand extensions under the same image; with the creative team to discuss image and packaging development; and with the lawyers and accountants to protect the image and set budgets for image development.

You'll be familiar with trademark and copyright law and be continually on the lookout for anyone daring to infringe on your legally protected image. By working with the market research managers, you'll learn that customers have intuitive and irrational preferences; for example, people prefer magazines with blue or red covers and are less likely to buy a magazine with a green cover.

Branding is driven by **market segmentation**. So you may have a version of a product for a youth market which has a particular advertising and design strategy, while the same product can be rebranded for the **silver market** with a different advertising message and package design. With both groups, your objective is to create product prestige and meaningful social visibility.

You'll have to watch out for unfortunate associations which damage the brand and ensure that the name does not have unexpected connotations in foreign countries – there are dedicated third party agencies which specialise in brand names and brand registration.

Sometimes the **generic brands** are the bestsellers. Most of the supermarkets, for example, have 'own brand' products which are sold without frills and cheaply because allegedly no investment is made in advertising and promotion. In fact, many of these generic brands receive considerable promotion. The difference is that they are cheap and cheerful but just as good as their more expensive competitors. Many supermarket own-brand cosmetics, for example, are virtually the same as expensive luxury cosmetics 10 or 20 times the price.

Brand managers frequently engage in a **battle of the brands**, in which fairly similar products are set head to head against each other in an attempt to capture the hearts and minds of a target audience. Coca-Cola and Pepsi, for example, and Levi and Lee Cooper, are often seen directly and aggressively competing.

There is huge investment in branding – quite rightly, because it can mean that a product sinks like a stone or flies into the top-selling list and stays there. When BP Amoco devised a logo to replace the BP shield, it invested £136 million in design and promotion. So everyone in marketing takes brand management very seriously and the brand manager has an important job to do.

Skills you'll need

■ You'll have to manage a budget, so financial skills should come naturally. 'Along with being able to read a balance sheet, you'll have to be able to understand research statistics, charts and graphs,' says Steve Phillips.

■ You'll need to be creative and articulate and have a finger on the pulse of what appeals to each market segment and the target consumer for each brand and product.

■ You'll have to be assertive in meetings with the market research, advertising, promotion and PR people, to make sure that they understand the brand associations you are trying to get across and use all their skills to promote and develop the brand in the way you want it developed.

■ You'll have to understand the psychology of customers and what makes people choose one product over another according to their 'feelings' as well as their experiences.

■ Your understanding of web marketing will have to be good. These days, running a website includes sponsorship, banner advertising and other promotional activities, which all have to be linked to the brand management.

Tips

■ Look at the ways in which brands are developed and new products launched under existing brands. It most frequently happens in the confectionery industry, so notice how old products are relaunched with new packaging, old sweets appear in a fresh flavour branded as 'new' and simple changes to product design or image stimulate an entire new advertising and promotion campaign. Next time you buy your favourite confectionery, look at how the packaging has changed since you first bought it. Don't limit yourself to just one product area – the same exercise is undertaken with cars, washing machines, washing powder, computers, pizzas and dog food. See if you can identify what the brand managers have done and judge whether they have been successful in their endeavours.

■ Try to think of new ways in which your favourite food could be branded and the brand developed. What name would you give your favourite home-cooked supper, for example, and how could it be changed to create a new product in a few months' time?

- Ask your friends what they think of when you mention certain well-known consumer brands to them. The adjectives they use might include 'safe', 'quality' and 'reliable', while others might provoke 'tasteless', 'boring' or 'conventional' – not all brand images are as positive as the brand managers would like.

Glossary

- **Battle of the brands**
  When manufacturers, dealers and retailers of different brands of similar products enter into a price- or promotion-based competition to win the greatest market share.
- **Brand extension**
  A strategy for exploiting a brand by adding new variations of products or services.
- **Generic brands**
  Items which promote the names of products rather than the name of the vendor or manufacturer.
- **Market segmentation**
  The process of subdividing a market into distinct subsets of customers who behave in similar ways and have similar values, incomes or needs.
- **Silver market**
  Retired people or people over 50 years old. Also known as the grey market (not to be confused with the grey market of illicit unauthorised products) and embracing silver surfers – retired people who use the internet.

Campaign executive

See *Project or campaign manager*.

Channel marketing manager

Money: Medium. Up to £45,000 with some seven years' experience in marketing, but you're likely to start on £16,000 as a junior in a marketing department.

Hours: The more senior you get, the more unstructured and longer your hours become.

Health risk: Low, except for the stress of long hours.

Pressure rating: Medium to high. The worst risk is upsetting the distributors, but keeping them happy while still reaching the widest potential customer base can be impossible.

Glamour rating: Low. Not many people even know what a channel marketing manager is, yet some say it's the best job in marketing because it's so hands-on.

Travel rating: Medium. You may have to go to exhibitions and shows as well as visit the firm's partners and distributors, but all the travel will definitely be work related.

'Channel' refers to the route to market, which varies from client to client. Some vendors sell direct to their customers, while others sell only through third-party resellers or distributors, who may in turn sell to retailers who sell on to users at the end of the chain. Some firms have mixed channel strategies, while others are conscientious about keeping a 'clean' channel and selling only through designated partners. Each channel model requires a different marketing and PR approach and channel marketing is a specialist discipline.

Jo-Ann Prior works as channel marketing and PR manager within a large computer software vendor which also uses third-party agencies for some of its marketing and PR activities. She says that an understanding of the subtleties of the channel and the needs of all those operating within it is essential. 'When I first started I really didn't understand how the different partners interrelated and what their concerns were and I was on a very sharp learning curve for the first three months. Luckily, there was an outgoing channel marketing manager to show me the ropes and explain why some partners worked with us directly and why we had to be so careful not to sell direct to users.'

How to get into Marketing and PR

Jo-Ann's firm helps its channel partners with their marketing. 'A lot of my work is spending time with the partners like distributors and resellers and helping them with their strategies and plans,' she says. 'But I like that because it involves travelling around the country to meet them and organising road shows and seminars for them and their clients.'

Jo-Ann's job is extremely broad and she has responsibility for all aspects of marketing to and for the channel. 'My work includes advertising, PR and press relations work, devising sales promotions and direct mail campaigns and working on point-of-sale material too. I have to tackle every aspect of marketing and have different campaigns for different areas of the channel and different campaigns for our channel partner too. It sounds like I have to keep a lot of balls in the air at once and it feels like it too!'

But in spite of the fact that she is frequently extremely busy, even though she has an assistant to help her, Jo-Ann says that she loves her work. 'It's not just the campaigns and organisation which I love, it's the fact that I have to develop close working relationships with so many people, from those in the agencies which work for us, to the marketing people within our channel partners, and with the freelance people that we also use.

'My day starts with clearing my e-mail in-box and as I rarely get less than 30 every time I log on, that can take half an hour or so,' she says. 'I also have to liaise with all the product managers and the brand manager who is responsible for the overall corporate message.' Jo-Ann says that it can be difficult meeting the needs of all the different people involved. 'I try not to let things become driven by committees because then they get lost, so it is a matter of arriving at strategies which suit everyone without the objectives becoming diluted.'

The channel marketing manager gets to know the user community far more closely than a traditional marketing manager, says Jo-Ann. 'One of the things I really like about my job is that I've made so many good friends. We only have six distributors so I spend a lot of time with the marketing managers in those organisations and talk about how we can work together to persuade the resellers and users that buy from them to take our products.' She also spends time with some of the biggest user organisations, even though they don't actually buy their products from her. 'We have some really big organisations among our customers and we have to persuade them to stick with us and not go to our competitors, so I have to spend time wining and dining and entertaining them and hearing how they'd like to see the products improved.'

Jo-Ann says that channel marketing has changed since the Internet arrived and became a force in sales and marketing. 'At one time we could easily keep our channel really clean, but these days customers expect to be able to buy direct from us and it is harder to refer them to our distributors or retailers. We wouldn't mind, but the trouble is that our competitors are going direct and selling over the web and so we've got to do the same.'

Jo-Ann had five years' experience as a marketing assistant and then a marketing manager before moving over to channel marketing. 'You need to have a good understanding of all the different strands of marketing, so it is rarely a first job,' she says. But she recommends it for someone looking for a dynamic, fun and active job with lots of responsibility.

Skills you'll need

- Foreign languages are increasingly essential, says Jo-Ann. 'We are moving into a pan-European distribution model,' she says, 'and although we have been using third parties to do some of the negotiations we really have to have our own discussions with our local **agents** and distributors in France, Germany, Spain and Italy.' Jo-Ann speaks fluent French but has only rusty German and Spanish. 'I'm taking night classes,' she says, 'but I wish I spent more time on languages while I was at school.'
- You'll need diplomacy and tact and the ability to deal with all levels and types of managers, from creative artistic designers to product managers and technology geeks.

Tips

- Get a good grounding in all the marketing disciplines and if you can't decide which one you like best, go for a job as a channel marketer because you'll be expected to use them all, not specialise in one or two. Look for channel publications, which are those aimed at and read only by the distributors, dealers and others in the delivery chain.

Glossary

- **Agents**
  Wholesalers who do not take title of the goods and are rewarded through a commission or fee.

Communications manager

See *Marcoms manager.*

Consumer affairs specialist

Money:	Up to £25,000 a year, possibly with some perks like membership of a health club or a subsidised canteen.
Hours:	Usually conventional 10–6 with an hour for lunch. There's seldom a need to work overtime.
Health risk:	Low.
Pressure rating:	If you have the temperament to deal with angry and irate people, or thrive on it, you won't feel much stress or pressure, but if you are highly strung or sensitive you might find that the work starts to get to you after a while.
Glamour rating:	Low to medium.
Travel rating:	Low. You'll rarely travel anywhere other than to commute home.

You might call this the 'front end' of marketing. It involves working closely with customers, often when they have problems, to repair any damage to the brand and to get feedback about the product or services and how they can be improved.

When Sarah McDowell took a job in a call centre to help finance her way through university, she had no idea that it would lead to a career in marketing and consumer affairs, but it did. She explains, 'When I was at university I was desperate for money and the only respectable well-paid part-time work I could find was working on a call centre help desk, for a company which provided those services for their customers. It was an outsourcing agency and I was helping people with problems with their computers. I didn't know much about computers, but it was all about registering the call, making nice noises, finding out what was wrong and then passing the call on to the appropriate technical person.' Sarah's employers realised that she had a real ability to calm agitated and angry people, and when she left university they offered her a job in their marketing department. 'I was doing an English degree and they seemed to think that I had the right skills for a career in marketing. I was interested, but got a proper postgraduate qualification in marketing before I started work – and then I joined a proper marketing agency and didn't stay with the call centre.'

After a year in the marketing agency working on general marketing jobs for clients, Sarah applied for a job as a consumer affairs specialist for a health foods products vendor. She says, 'My job now has its roots in marketing and I have to come up with some new marketing, PR and promotional ideas and see them through, but my main job is as first point of contact within the company for customers with problems or concerns.'

She is now studying psychology with the Open University, partly because she believes in lifelong learning and partly because she knows it will be useful in her work. 'I want to know more about why customers make purchasing decisions, what they buy and when and how those things can be affected.'

In some businesses this role is called PR, but Sarah believes that by focusing on the customers and their needs and problems, she is better able to conceive marketing strategies that will really appeal directly to the customers. She says, 'Advertising and marketing are all very well, but you still need to persuade customers to buy your products when they go into a store or on-line. By keeping in close contact with them and listening to what they are saying, I think that I am able to tailor the marketing and sales activity more accurately.'

By keeping in touch with customers and being the first to hear their concerns and views, Sarah says she is able to gather information which is useful for other marketing professionals within the organisation. 'Sometimes it is the point-of-sale material, other times it is the packaging or a television advert. They will tell me their views and I can pass them on to the creative teams responsible.'

Resolving customer issues before they become major problems also helps preserve the image of the brand. Sarah says, 'As we sell health foods we are very dependent on views, fashions, trends and propaganda, and word-of-mouth recommendations are very important reinforcements of the traditional advertising and promotion. By keeping an ear close to the ground and knowing what customers are saying we can keep closely in touch with the way the brand and products are being talked about.'

A typical day for Sarah involves spending at least an hour every morning on the Internet, dealing with e-mails from customers and retailers. 'Then I return a lot of phone calls and have to deal with any problems that have arisen since the day before. The afternoon is often spent in meetings with marketing and creative people, but I am always available to take a call from a customer.'

Sarah recently had to deal with a problem batch of pills which were contaminated. 'There was no real health risk to customers, but those who took them found that their skin turned a peculiar shade of orange. We had bought the pills from the Far East and repackaged them and it was my job to take the calls of complaint and answer letters and e-mails. Then I worked with the external PR agency about how we should deal with the situation so that we were not damaged. I also helped the marketing people devise a short-term campaign which capitalised on the situation, rather than just ignoring it. At the end of the day we turned the situation into a positive one and the brand emerged with a strong sense of responsibility towards the community. It turned out very well for us.'

Sarah also sometimes gets involved with focus groups to help develop new products and decide on new names and target audiences. 'We are also using technology by having webcams at the points of purchase and asking customers for feedback about their views on the products, telling us why they bought them. That information is getting passed back to product development and the advertising professionals. By taking this proactive approach, we have a definite advantage over our competitors,' she says.

Not all firms have a consumer affairs person in the marketing department, but Sarah says that it is a growing trend, as a response to the growth in customer empowerment. 'The Internet in particular has given consumers more power and choice and it is important to keep in touch with the consumer pull on sales.'

She loves her work, she says, because it brings her into such close contact with the customers. 'When I was a little girl my mother was sure I was going to be an air hostess or a nurse because of the games I played, but this is much better. It pays more, for one thing!'

Skills you'll need

- Brilliant interpersonal skills, including tact, diplomacy and charm. Sarah says, 'Often the people I talk to are irate or upset, so I have to calm them down before sorting out the problem. Then I have to do reports and pass back my views to the relevant people within the organisation who I think would do well to know what customers are thinking.'
- Sarah also has to be creative, thinking up new campaigns and working with the project and marketing managers to see campaigns through.
- She speaks three languages, which she says is very helpful because the firm sells across Europe and she has to deal with customers in other regions as well as the UK.
- 'I also have to know about the user end of an IT system,' she says, 'although I don't have to have any technical knowledge.'

■ Sarah doubts that anyone can learn the kind of intuitive skills that a consumer affairs manager needs, but says that you work at developing whatever customer-focused skills you might have. 'Be honest but tactful in all your dealings with friends and colleagues,' she says. 'Ask questions but be careful not to upset people.'

■ She also advises that you practise being friendly and smiling and be as enthusiastic as possible about everything you do and everything that those around you do.

Copywriter

Money: Up to £24,000. Definitely a job to keep the wolf from the door, not to get rich.

Hours: Regular, although you may find yourself thinking of projects you're working on at home or while doing other things.

Health risk: Low.

Pressure rating: Medium to high. You'll often have to work to deadlines.

Glamour rating: Medium. Writers are often the great unsung heroes of marketing campaigns.

Travel rating: Low.

Someone has to write all the words that appear on sales promotional material and packages. And it is more of a skill than many realise.

Adam Thornley really wants to be a novelist, but rather than starve in a garret he is pragmatic enough to realise that he has to have a 'proper' job while he waits for a publisher to accept his first novel. Being a marketing copywriter is better than most jobs, because he is working with words and forever practising his art, even if it is not as creative as he would like. He says, 'Sometimes I get fed up with writing slogans and catchy words for advertisements, but I usually get over it.'

Adam has a reputation for being difficult, but his colleagues in the marketing agency where he works put it down to his creative temperament. He is also extremely good at thinking of exactly the right words to use to create a mood or encourage people to buy a new product or switch from their old brand. His boss says, 'I wouldn't want to encourage anyone thinking of becoming a copywriter that it is all right to be awkward, but I know that Adam gets quite down sometimes and he is such a good writer when he is on form that it is worth putting up with his moods.'

Adam sometimes has to deal with clients and goes to client meetings to take a brief, but usually just sits quietly while others in the marketing team do the talking. He says, 'My job is definitely a case of little is more. If I was paid by the number of words I wrote I'd be the cheapest person on the team. I often have to think of a two- or three-word slogan or a six- or ten-word strapline and that's all I'll do in a day. But writing is not something that can be done to order and sometimes I think of the best captions or titles or slogans out of work, like in the bath or in bed.'

Adam also has to write user manuals and instructions, and as the agency he works for has a wide variety of clients he can find himself writing all kinds of material. 'Last week I had to do a user manual for a washing machine and this week it is the words for a point-of-sale competition for a new brand of toothpaste. I'm also working on a script for a television advert and one of our clients is building a new website and I have to write several pages for it.' Such variety appeals to Adam, although he complains that at the end of the day he has no creative energy left to work on his next novel. 'My first one is with a publisher at the moment and I am hoping for a deal, but the fact is that very few writers earn a living from novels. Most writers have to have a proper job as well and this one is better than selling media space or being a sales representative.'

Skills you'll need

- Good English and creative writing skills.
- Adam has to interpret the client briefing and translate what they want into language that is suitable for the media and appeals to the prospective audience. 'I have to be a message interpreter,' he says, 'turning what the client and other marketing professionals say into words that will capture the hearts and minds of the customers.'
- Foreign languages are very useful too, says Adam, but IT skills other than word processing are unnecessary. 'I have to know how to use a computer but not how to programme or manage one,' he says.

Tips

- Write as much as you can. Adam recommends that you use pen and paper rather than a word processor. 'It's too easy to make changes on a word processor,' he says. 'Trying to get the right words first time is good practice.'

Creative designer / director

Money: At this level, £50,000 would be the minimum. Income can easily reach six figures.

Hours: Flexible. You can set your own hours to a large extent, which probably means you work longer days than many others.

Health risk: Low.

Pressure rating: Medium to high. You will probably have overall responsibility for campaigns, at least for the creative side, and if anything goes wrong with any aspect, the buck will stop with you.

Glamour rating: Medium to high, depending on whether the agency has a high profile and what sort of clients you have.

Travel rating: Medium. You'll probably be largely office based, but there could also be plenty of opportunities for UK and international travel. Again, it depends on exactly who you work for and what clients you have.

The creative director oversees the art department, pulls together the work of the visual and writing teams and looks at the best way to get the message to the audience.

Maud Steinberg is the senior creative director for a leading New York-based marketing agency, although she works in the London office. The client base includes a leading international conglomerate with a wide range of different food and **FMCG** brands and product sets, plus other global companies, including a computer hardware vendor. She says, 'When a client has a lot of different products and there are many routes to market and ways of marketing and advertising, there needs to be someone keeping an umbrella view over the whole thing to make sure that everything is on message.'

Maud's job involves regular meetings with the clients plus regular and routine meetings with the creative heads of all departments and outside agencies to ensure that there is co-ordination between them. 'It would be very easy for duplication to happen, or cross-overs between the brands, or for the brand messages to be inadvertently confused,' she says. 'My job is to make sure that everything remains clear and the best marketing media are used in every instance.'

She is involved in preparing the briefing documents which go to the art and copywriting teams and synchronising the strategies which the project and campaign managers go ahead and implement.

Maud studied art, psychology and philosophy at university and then did a year's postgraduate marketing course before starting work with a small agency, where she was able to learn and practise all the different skills required for marketing and PR. 'My favourite job was working with the media and journalists,' she says, 'and at one time I considered a career in PR, but my first love has always been art and creative design.' In her spare time Maud does pottery and watercolours and has won several competitions.

'I also have an interest in the power of the Internet and the way that e-commerce is changing the way we do business, so my current job pulls together all my interests,' she says.

The only part of the job that Maud dislikes is all the meetings. 'Sometimes they seem to go on for ever and get nowhere, but we have to sit through them and keep concentrating. I'm expected to come up with suggestions and make reports and analysis reviews afterwards, so I have to keep focused,' she says. 'I have to do management jobs but I really prefer the creative work.'

What Maud really likes is keeping an eye on new technology and looking at how it can be incorporated into the creative techniques that her agency uses. 'It's all about keeping ahead of other agencies in the innovative use of technology. It's amazing how quickly a new good idea gets picked up by other agencies, and before you know it everyone is doing it. Part of my job is to stay one step ahead and anticipate new developments and see how they can be used creatively as part of the strategy to deliver the message.'

Maud is currently looking at **WAP technology** and how mobile phones and other hand-held devices can receive marketing messages and slogans. 'We are working with a wireless company at building small displays into all kinds of consumer goods, such as luggage and clothing, so that advertisers can send messages in all kinds of novel ways,' she says.

Maud also looks backwards all the time – to see how old fonts and processing techniques, for example, can be revived and integrated into new campaigns. 'There is always a place for the retro in marketing, although the trick is sometimes in how to integrate it so that it has a modern look and feel.'

Sometimes controlling headstrong creative types can be a challenge, but Maud says that her psychology background comes in very useful. 'I think that tact and diplomacy and the art of managing people can be learned and by understanding people's responses to certain situations I like to think that I can get them to do what I want most of the time.'

Despite her dislike of meetings and management, Maud is very good at both. She is able to control a meeting that she has called and contribute to meetings in which strong-minded and opinionated marketing professionals are determined to get their way. 'Sometimes meetings with clients can be quite fiery,' she says. 'They often have their views on what they want while we know that there are better, more effective and efficient ways to get their message across. Part of my job is explaining how the whole marketing package works together and that elements can't be considered in isolation.'

Maud has a clear idea of how she wants her career to develop. She says, 'I am determined to have my own agency and I already have two other experienced marketing professionals and an accountant organised and ready to make the break from their existing jobs.' She needs investment, however, to get premises and make them suitable and to last through the first year when clients may be thin on the ground. 'We are talking to some investors but it would be better if we had the money ourselves.' She is confident, however, that if she can find the funding, she will be able to launch an impressive and innovative agency. 'I have so many ideas and my colleagues are so good at their own areas of specialisation that I'm sure we will be very successful,' she says.

Skills you'll need

- Maud's background of a combination of art, psychology, philosophy and marketing is perfect for the complex multifaceted job of creative director. She also has the experience and presence to generate respect for her views. This is not a job for school-leavers or graduates, but is something to be aimed at as a career objective.
- Any skills and experience that you can pick up, such as technology and IT, foreign languages, management and marketing, will be useful. As you go through your early career, you also need to build a reputation for creativity, responsibility and vision.

Tips

- Being a creative director involves taking an overall view of several different elements of a marketing campaign, so work at seeing the bigger picture and not getting too bogged down in one aspect of whatever you're doing.
- Work at getting along with people; don't make enemies if you can avoid it.

How to get into Marketing and PR

■ **FMCG**

Fast-moving consumer goods, which includes products like washing powder and foods.

■ **WAP technology**

Wireless application protocol, likely to be the biggest leap in communications since the advent of the mobile phone. It allows individuals to log onto the Internet from any location, using their mobile or desktop PC, accessing data that may be personally tailored.

Customer relationship manager

See *Relationship marketing manager*.

Customer service manager

Money: After four years in marketing you might expect to earn £28,000. As team leader you'll get some perks, like a company car and gym membership. If you want to earn more then you might have to think about moving sideways into another job in marketing.

Hours: Customer service departments are commonly open from 8.30 a.m. until 8 p.m. from Monday to Friday and teams take turns to work early and late shifts.

Health risk: Low.

Pressure rating: Medium, or high if you get upset and angry with irate and rude callers.

Glamour rating: Low, but customer service is a vital part of the marketing machine and a valuable opportunity to change customers' perceptions and views.

Travel rating: Low, although you may have on-site meetings with clients.

Unlike the customer relationship manager, who is thinking of new ways in which the client can work more closely with the existing and new customer base, the customer service manager has to deal with problems as they arise. He or she is in charge of the support or help desk, which is usually a telecentre with all operatives on the phone all day.

If there is any job in marketing that needs the patience of a saint, it is that of customer service manager. Lucia Jefferson says that she loves the work, but it is not everyone's idea of a good job. 'The trouble is that no one ever contacts the customer service manager to tell them how happy they are. Everyone we come into contact with has a problem and they are often very angry by the time we get to speak to them,' she says. Lucia studied English literature with psychology at university and then did a year's postgraduate marketing training because she thought she'd like marketing as a career. 'I started in customer service for a computer company because I couldn't find a job in mainstream marketing, and I've been here ever since. It is the best part of marketing, as far as I'm concerned, because I like dealing with people and problems. It suits me, although it does stress me out sometimes. I like that, though, and it is extremely satisfying when someone who started off with a problem ends up being pleased and happy and feeling good about the company.'

Lucia sees her job as an opportunity to convert negative messages into positive ones. 'We contact people three months after they originally called us, to make sure that everything is working properly. It only takes a moment but the long-term benefit is immeasurable. We have a reputation now as a caring IT company, which is a pretty rare thing, I can tell you!'

She says that many IT companies try to initiate effective customer support but fail. 'The main reason is the attitude of the people at the end of the telephones. You have to be calm and reassuring and be able to develop people's confidence that you can resolve this problem and will look after them in the future.'

Although many of the calls are about technical problems, Lucia has very limited in-depth technical knowledge. Neither does she look for technical expertise in those she recruits. 'That can always be learned or I can always find someone who understands the technical details. What are far more important are people skills and the attitude and approach of the tele-operative.'

Lucia is responsible for writing the scripts for the customer service agents. This means she has to anticipate all the questions and problems that might arise and devise the answer which best helps communicate the company's message. She says, 'My psychology background comes in very useful in knowing the best thing to say to help the situation.'

Lucia continues, 'Some customer service people seem to think that the problem belongs to the customer, but I think that it belongs to us and that's what makes the difference. It's all about reassuring and taking ownership of the problem.'

Lucia passes reports on the calls to the product manager and to outside agencies. 'We want to avoid one or two problems becoming a stream, so as soon as we get more than a couple of similar problems it gets referred to the research and development people so they can see whether there is a design problem that they can help improve.'

Lucia works with the training department to make sure that the customer service staff are properly trained in all new technologies. They also receive 'soft skill' training to make sure that they are as customer friendly as possible, and repeat the training on a regular basis. 'I like people to feel that they are privileged to be helping people, and to enjoy making the customers feel good when they deal with us.'

Lucia uses IT to help create scripts for the tele-operatives and to keep records on all calls. Service staff are then prompted by the system with the right thing to say and when to call back to make sure that everything is working properly. 'The system also has an intelligent expert system which recognises free English text and will sort records according to the type of call or the source of the problem. We can also see where they bought their system from, to see if we can help prevent problems by providing better on-the-ground help. As a result of these reports we now give in-store salespeople better training.

'This is a communication job,' says Lucia. 'You've got to like people and you've got to like the human race at its worst. If you do, then you can get a lot of job satisfaction and make some good friends.' She says that it is important that the whole department works well together, so they go out for regular 'bonding' outings, in the evenings and at weekends. 'We all take our partners and have a good time, and it helps us work better together.'

Skills you'll need

- Customer service is part of communications marketing and good relationships with callers need to be established as quickly as possible – poor ones will send you down faster than you could believe. If there is one thing that marks out good customer service people, even above other marketing professionals, it is their ability to know intuitively what each customer needs and to calm them down even before starting to resolve the problem. Good people skills are necessary in any job in marketing, but in customer support they are critical.
- Customer service marketing professionals also have to be able to interpret technical issues in non-technical terms and, conversely, to translate a caller's problem into technical terms. Often the customer is unintentionally misleading, perhaps being convinced that the problem lies in one place when it is in fact located elsewhere. 'Tact and communications skills are all,' says Lucia. She also has to be able to empathise with callers' situations, yet still be able to promote the firm's message.
- Lucia's psychology degree is undoubtedly standing her in very good stead, but sales training would also be useful in understanding people's actions and working out your responses.
- Languages are mandatory for Lucia's department, but often essential in most other companies too. Lucia says, 'Our computers are sold all over the world and the ability to deal with angry and upset people talking French or German is all part of the job.'
- Lucia needs to understand how to use the Internet to provide customer service and help. She says, 'The Internet site is available 24 hours a day and seven days a week, and a lot of customers now use that when they have a problem. It requires a different sort of response, but all the same

principles apply.'The Internet also helps by dealing with the most common problems.'We have a frequently asked questions area where people can see the common problems and learn how to resolve them themselves, thus saving our operatives for the worst problems.'

- Practise explaining complex things in simple terms, both in verbal descriptions and written explanations. You have to be able to interpret and convey situations while maintaining accuracy and courtesy.
- Practise keeping your cool when faced with hostility and criticism.'You have to remember that no one is usually antagonistic for the sake of it and they often have good reason for being angry,' Lucia says.
- If you have problems with products, try telephoning their customer service help desks and see for yourself what makes a good one and what makes a bad one. Think how you like to be treated when you are the unhappy customer.

Direct marketing manager

Money: Expect £24,000 after three years in the job; up to £45,000 if you progress to be the most senior member of the direct marketing team. The only way you will earn more is by launching your own agency.

Hours: Normally 10–6, but longer if evening meetings with clients are involved.

Health risk: Low.

Pressure rating: Medium. There are two main pressures: to come up with new ideas, and to make sure that campaigns are executed efficiently.

Glamour rating: Low. Direct marketing still has a bad reputation and even in professional marketing circles is not regarded particularly well.

Travel rating: Low, other than for occasional travel to client sites for meetings or to see designers or printers. Most of your work will be done from the office, especially since the growth of the Internet.

Once, direct marketing meant approaching potential and existing customers via the telephone and mail, but these days the Internet is also included. Direct marketing managers have to know all about using the Internet as a tool if they are to make sure their companies stay ahead.

Lucy Earnshaw says that direct mailers have been accused of lacking imagination, but now they are demonstrating as much innovation as any other marketing specialist. She says, 'When I started in direct marketing eight years ago, I have to confess that most direct marketing was mail shots from the financial sector, holiday firms or home improvement companies and many were very dull and predictable. They were often very badly written and designed and must have been an enormous waste of money.'

Now, says Lucy, direct marketing is far more complex and refined. 'In the old days it was not unusual to have people transferred from the credit control department or stationery office into responsibility for direct mail. Now it is an integrated part of marketing strategies and earning the respect it deserves.'

The predictable old mail shots have largely been replaced by more attractive, better designed and worded items, although Lucy says that many of the financial companies are constrained by legislation.

These days, direct marketing is not just a one-way process. You don't simply send out a load of leaflets and hope someone – anyone – picks them up and responds. Increasingly, there is an interactive element. This is obvious with **telemarketing**, when potential customers are called by a telemarketing or sales operative. A conversation will develop, which will hopefully culminate in a request for more information or even a sale. Direct mail, including leafleting, invites interaction and response, but the response is less immediate. The Internet sits between the two, as a medium that invites response in the target audience's own time, as direct mail does, but with a conversation, as with the telephone.

All three methods can be closely targeted, although they depend heavily on database technology. As direct marketing manager you'd have to understand the fundamentals of how databases work and keep up with the latest technology, including aspects such as data storage and retrieval. Dan Rudler is a direct marketing executive with 12 years' experience behind him. He started when direct mail and telesales were the only techniques available, but has since become an expert on using the Internet for direct marketing. 'It is amazing how precisely we can target the customers and how much we can know about each one, their preferences and past purchasing history,' he says.

Increasingly, direct marketing is becoming more innovative too. 'At one time the most innovative thing was to offer a prize for anyone who replied to a direct mail or leaflet inserted into a magazine, like the *Reader's Digest* prizes. These days we have to be much more creative about encouraging people to reply so that we can find out more about them and store their details.'

The law stipulates that people have to agree to be targeted by direct mail and Internet **spam mail** and people have the option of having their names deleted from mailing lists. This means that marketers have to make sure that their mailings are not irritating or offensive, so that as few people as possible want to be excluded.

Mailing lists are bought from specialist list agencies, and large agencies and consultancies have specialist list managers who do nothing but manage, clean and maintain old lists and purchase new lists (see *List manager*). But Dan says that in many cases the direct marketing manager also has to be the list manager: 'It's part of my job.'

Lucy says that direct marketing is sometimes so subtle that it does not even mention the brand or product, at least overtly. 'We recently handled a direct marketing campaign for a car company which focused on the **lifestyle** issues. Through a mail shot and a direct Internet campaign, we were able to generate very good return on investment for the customer.'

Lucy also works with magazine and pack inserts, point-of-sale promotions and teleselling. 'Direct marketing is far wider than most people understand,' she says. 'I'm going for a special diploma in direct marketing and I really enjoy the specialisation.' Lucy works in an agency that deals only in direct marketing commissions and she says she enjoys thinking up novel and interesting campaigns. 'Even if the method is tried and tested, like direct mail, we can still be innovative and interesting,' she says.

Lucy spends some time working on new ideas for campaigns, but most of her day is dedicated to chasing printers, designer and copywriters and liaising with clients. 'You have to be good at communicating ideas and managing clients. They all want immediate results and you have to manage their expectations.'

Skills you'll need

- Number one is creativity.
- You need to understand how marketing techniques can be interrelated and how to build a brand on the web. Traditional brand literacy and segmentation skills are needed to develop integrated direct marketing campaigns, based on an understanding of customer preferences and behaviour. You have to know how to exploit the new opportunities that the Internet and digital media have created. Lucy says, 'The Internet has radically extended the marketer's ability to understand customers and the way in which they relate to and derive value from brands.'
- Diplomacy and tact are valuable and it helps to be charming and persuasive.

Tips

- Creativity can easily be stifled by a conservative approach, so make sure that you opt to work for a firm that encourages and supports unusual ideas and gives you the freedom to express them.

Glossary

- **Lifestyle**
  The patterns of taste, living and consumption of individuals and groups of individuals which affect buying and consumption.
- **Spam mail**
  Unsolicited marketing information sent by e-mail. The origins of the term are unclear, but are probably something to do with the ubiquitous pink luncheon meat which at one

time appeared in salads everywhere. A spam list is created from marketing and direct sales lists. Individuals can arrange to have their names removed from such lists.

■ **Telemarketing**
Using the telephone to sell direct to consumers.

Display creator / manager

See *Point-of-sale merchandiser*.

E-commerce marketing manager

Money: Expect £17,000 as a starting salary as a junior. You can work your way up to around £48,000 with profit shares and other perks like a company car, health insurance and gym membership.

Hours: Fairly regular, even though the Internet is a **24/7/365** environment.

Health risk: Low.

Pressure rating: Low, although if you find marketing hard, are not a natural communicator and don't like technology you might find it stressful.

Glamour rating: Medium. Anything connected with the Internet has a high glamour rating at the moment, but expect some mundane moments.

Travel rating: Low. The Internet, with voice and video transmissions, means that travel is irrelevant.

As the Internet has grown and e-business has flourished, despite a few well-publicised company crashes, a new job has evolved, usually called e-commerce marketing manager. Most conventional marketing managers are having to understand e-commerce as well, however, and integrate it into their jobs.

Bill Hannaford started his career in advertising after doing business studies at university. He became interested in exploiting the Internet for advertising, using banner ads, site sponsorship and product promotion. He says, 'Then I took a job as an e-commerce marketing manager with a book retailer and frankly I learned a lot on the job. It was more important to have traditional marketing skills rather than Internet skills. Everyone is learning and not many people have much track record because the Internet is so new.'

Now Bill works for an e-tailing business which sells books over the Internet. He says, 'The most important part to concentrate on is fulfilment and delivery. I also have to devise the on-site strategies and incentives to get people to bookmark the site.'

He is very conscious that web shoppers are only two clicks away from a competitor and that the Internet is still having to compete with 'bricks and mortar' businesses. 'When it comes to clothes, for example, people still like to try things on. But it is getting easier, provided they have confidence in the site.'

Site security is crucial, so that people will give their credit card numbers for an on-site transaction. 'Part of building the electronic brand is to ensure that people trust the site and will give their credit card details without worrying. That confidence is part of the brand message and we work very hard to make sure that transactions are secure and orders are processed efficiently.'

Bill says, 'The firm I work for had not been involved with the Internet until pressure from other booksellers forced them to look at it. They were very late to the party.' He was involved in reorganising all the processes within the company so that the business was optimised to take full advantage of electronic sales. He says, 'Now, when customers order books from our site, an order is automatically placed with our suppliers so that we are restocked. That makes us more efficient and means we can reduce our stockholding.

'I have also been looking at different forms of **push marketing**, which means that once people have bought from us we will automatically e-mail them every month to tell them of new books we are offering in the same area. We know what they are probably interested in and can send them ideas for books that we think will interest them, based on their past orders.'

The company is also looking at extending its range, and as Internet marketing manager, Bill has been involved with those decisions. 'We already sell videos and some magazines, but we are looking at some **brand extension** into new markets, and also so that we get more business from our existing client base. We are looking at sports clothing and some household goods. I'm working with a market research agency on what types of products we should sell and the messages that should go alongside each product.'

Bill will have to write a report and recommendation for the board and then develop brands and strategies for each new product. 'In many ways Internet marketing is just the same as traditional marketing, but there are some very important differences. One is the attention span of the site visitor, which means that the copy on the site pages has to be sharply written and concise; the other is the technical limitations, which means that if the site is too complex, people don't wait for it to download.'

E-commerce marketing is also linked to other activities within the firm. 'We also have to make sure that the website address is on all products and marketing materials and try to promote the product in conventional ways such as traditional magazine advertising and PR. I work with other marketing professionals and outside agencies to achieve that, but it is my job to make sure that everything is properly integrated.'

The e-commerce activities also have to be integrated with the back- and front-office IT systems, and although there is an IT manager who takes care of the nuts and bolts of integration, it is up to Bill to make sure that the supply chain is working as efficiently as possible. 'My job involves lots of liaising between different departments and looking for new ideas for promotion and marketing over the web. We are now looking at incentives for customers which can be reclaimed as cash, and competitions over the web, which apparently are very effective.'

Bill says he likes working at the front line of marketing and technology. 'We are partly adapting the old ways of working and partly thinking of completely new ways of marketing. Some of it is trial and error. We will make mistakes, but every now and again we will think of something that will really boost sales and help get the brand messages across.'

For the long term, Bill thinks that he might start his own agency helping small and medium businesses to sell and market on-line. 'I think there is a limit to the amount I can earn with this job title and the next step is to become self-employed. I'm currently looking for a web page designer and a financial person to get a balanced team, but it takes a special sort of person who can think outside the box and is prepared to take a gamble on launching a business.'

Skills you'll need

- Marketing expertise and experience are essential, but so is an understanding of the technical potential and limitations of the Internet and e-business. Bill says,' I don't have to actually understand programming, but I do have to know the processes and products which will allow on-line selling to be really effective.'
- People skills, as you'll have to deal with a lot of other managers from outsourced delivery firms, as well as site designers, advertising marketing professionals and others.
- Languages are useful but not essential as English is the lingua franca of the Internet.

Tips

- To be an e-commerce marketing manager you need to keep an eye on two areas – marketing and Internet technology – and the sooner you start the better. The best way to understand web marketing is to be a web surfer and experience it as an end-user. Surf the web as often as you can and note the advertisements and promotions, and asking yourself what catches your eye and what turns you off.

- **24/7/365**

  Continuously, 24 hours a day, 7 days a week and 365 days a year.

- **Brand extension**

  A strategy for exploiting a brand by adding new variations of products or services.

- **Push marketing**

  Taking the initiative to the potential or existing customer to persuade them that this is something they want and need, rather than waiting for the customer to go looking for it. Often utilises mobile phone and e-mail technology.

Exhibitions and seminars organiser

Money: Expect to start on around £12,000, rising to £45,000 when you are a well-established and highly regarded exhibition organiser. There are sometimes perks like a company car and discounted travel and clothing, and often products are disposed of after events have finished and you may be able to pick up many display or demonstration products very cheaply.

Hours: Long; 9–7 is not unusual, or later when an exhibition is imminent.

Health risk: Low.

Pressure rating: High. But if you love what you are doing, the pressure seems lower. There is also a great sense of relief when events are finished.

Glamour rating: Medium. It depends on the subject of the exhibition or seminar, but generally exhibition marketing is not fantastically glamorous.

Travel rating: Medium to high. A lot of time is spent in the office, but you may get to jet all over the world, visiting other exhibitions for ideas.

Exhibitions and seminars are an essential part of many marketing strategies, particularly for consumer products. There are computer shows, ideal home shows and specialist shows for all sectors and markets. Organising these events is a major logistical and planning exercise, and requires special skills and expertise.

Vicky Abbot works for a large marketing agency which has an exhibitions division, and she specialises in organising computer exhibitions. She says, 'Exhibitions had their heyday in the seventies and eighties and these days we are moving into the world of virtual exhibitions. However, there will also be a need for physical shows where people exhibit their products on stands and potential and existing customers come and see. Virtual shows are good, but you still want to touch and feel, and talk to the salespeople in person.'

Vicky's job involves organising and booking all the exhibitors, arranging the spaces they will each have, advertising and marketing the show and ensuring that visitors attend. There are often seminars at the shows, although Vicky also arranges separate seminars. 'When a company is promoting a new product, there is no better place than an exhibition where all their potential customers will be,' she says. 'I am definitely not an anorak – you don't have to understand computers to organise a computer show. In fact, I'm not really as computer literate as I should be, but I understand the power of technology and how it can be used to help in a conference context.

'I have to offer total management for the exhibitors, ensuring that messages are targeted and hit their audience. There is a lot of psychology involved, knowing what gets people to attend and then, once they are at the exhibition site, getting them to actually visit the stands.'

Vicky also arranges press conferences at the exhibitions, and personalised corporate events as side attractions to the main shows. She says, 'My job is split in several ways. First, I have to focus on attracting and signing up the exhibitors and then I have to organise the event itself. At the same time I have to concentrate on advertising and marketing the event so that visitors sign up, and to do that I have to arrange seminars that people will want to attend. That means approaching well-known and highly respected speakers or analysts who will make good presentations on topics that are of interest to the visitors.'

The problem is that Vicky has no control about what else is going on – other shows, rail strikes or bad weather. 'It can be an organisational nightmare,' she says.

She started working in the world of exhibitions straight from university and learned her marketing skills on the job. 'I was a junior assistant and had to do all the donkey work and boring jobs, but it is the best way to learn all about everything that needs doing.'

The job is largely project management, says Vicky. 'You have to be very well organised and I use project management software to help me. It alerts me when things are not done on time and threaten to hold up everything else.'

Creating the right type of environment for both exhibitors and visitors is a daunting task, but it is critical to the success of an event. 'A third of first-time exhibitors fail to repeat the experience,' says Vicky. 'The problem is that many shows fail to deliver. You have to have an original mind and be able to come up with some novel ideas without being too outlandish.'

Vicky has to work with a wide range of third parties as well as exhibitors, speakers and visitors. 'There are those who build the stands, the promoters and advertisers, the PR and press people and those who staff the stands. A single exhibition can involve months of work and hundreds of people.'

Vicky says she loves her job because it is so high-pressured and busy. 'I hardly get any time to myself,' she says.

'No sooner has one show finished than I have to start thinking about next year's event.' Over a year, Vicky is responsible for four different events, while her colleages handle smaller events. 'Every day is different,' she says, 'and involves so many different aspects of marketing. I love it because it is a real people job and has cycles and seasons to the work.'

Skills you'll need

- A calm, well-organised nature is essential, but knowing exactly how to plan and project manage an exhibition will be learned through experience. Vicky recommends her route into the industry, 'starting at the bottom'.
- Vicky learned three languages at school and they have proved very useful. 'Many of our exhibitors are from Europe and don't speak good English,' she says. 'I have a working knowledge of two languages and can get by in the third, but I wish I had more. I'm planning to start at night school to learn Russian and Chinese, because those countries are strong in exhibitions at the moment,' she says.
- As for technology, Vicky says her skills are very basic but adequate for her needs. 'I don't understand how technology works but I know how to make it do what I want it to do.' She uses word processing, e-mail and the Internet, but also has to plan virtual exhibitions. 'I have someone who understands more than I do who explains all that to me. My job is marketing, not technology,' she says.
- Sales and communications skills are essential. The rarity is finding someone who combines those attributes with the ability to plan projects. 'I have to be able to think of ten different things at once, keep six balls in the air and please a lot of different people all at the same time,' says Vicky, 'but I love it.'

Tips

- Project management can be practised and learned in many other tasks and jobs, including at school and university. Structure and plan your time, organise events in a methodical way, and be quietly well organised in everything you do.
- Learn from those around you about being organised.
- You need selling skills, so practise those, as well as communication skills and charm. All these can be practised at college or university by joining clubs, and making sure that your CV covers the range of your activities.

Film / video director

Money: You might have to work for less than £14,000 just to get the experience. This is an area where the number of people wanting to do the job far exceeds the number of jobs available, so you have to be prepared to accept anything to get you started. As an experienced director who has contact with clients you can expect to earn around £55,000.

Hours: Flexible. Can be from 7 in the morning until 9 or 10 at night, although there are periods in between projects when there is not much to do. Expect to work at home sometimes, preparing scripts and reports for clients.

Health risk: Low.

Pressure rating: Medium. If you love the work, the pressure is lower.

Glamour rating: High. Anything connected with the film industry is highly glamorous and working in the marketing industry means working on TV and cinema promos, pop promos and so forth.

Travel rating: Medium. You're likely to spend most of your time in the studio, but sometimes you'll need to visit clients or go on location for shoots.

Many firms want product videos or sales aids, while others want recorded demonstrations and customer testimonials. The techniques are not vastly different from creative film-making, but the money is a lot better.

When Sebastian French trained as a film-maker he had every intention of going to Hollywood and making blockbusters. He needed money to get there, however, so started a summer job working for an advertising agency in the film and video department. That was ten years ago and Seb hasn't been anywhere else, except on holiday. 'The trouble is that the work is fun and the money is good. I really enjoy it and I work with some great people and although I wanted to be a serious film-maker, the lure of regular good money was just too much.' Seb says that if the work was too awful or he'd had to compromise his integrity he wouldn't have stayed. 'Actually, the work is good fun and I get as much job satisfaction as in major movie-making without the insecurity.'

Sebastian's agency is a full-service marketing agency and handles advertising as well as PR, sales promotion, market research and e-commerce marketing. 'We will take over all aspects of marketing for our clients and we have departments in-house which are specialised in each of the marketing disciplines.' When a film is at the development stage, Seb has to work with the other departments. 'The idea is to get as much marketing and publicity mileage as possible, so we work together wherever we can.'

So the PR and publicity team will send out press releases promoting the film even before it is made, perhaps emphasising the individuals in it or the subject matter. 'One of our clients is a Far Eastern government department and we have to come up with lots of propaganda videos telling the population that they have to be good, honest citizens, watch out for their neighbours' property and not have loose morals. We have to write the scripts, cast and shoot the films, and it is extremely good fun and creatively satisfying,' says Seb.

Seb's department also has to produce very short videos for websites, and hour-long demonstrations of management techniques, again for public service bodies. 'The variety of work is extremely interesting,' says Seb. He is currently responsible for putting together the camera crews for each project and making sure that the props and wardrobe are ready when they are needed. 'I also do a bit of continuity work and act as best boy for the cameraman. In other words, I do a great variety of jobs on-set.'

The agency has a large basement room which is converted to a studio where Seb and his six colleagues work. 'On some projects there are an extra 10 or 15 others involved, as well as the actors. We have some favourites that we use whenever we can, while others we get from agencies,' he says. At any one time there are usually three or four projects on the go, at various stages of production.

'Because all our work is essentially marketing related, there is often a message that has to be conveyed in the script and the way that things are shot. The trick is to deliver on those expectations and at the same time make something that is entertaining to watch and creatively satisfying for us,' says Seb.

No one on Seb's team has got into the industry without going to film school, although Seb says that it does happen sometimes. 'I would recommend that anyone wanting to work in the movies, even marketing industry movies, gets a good degree and gets involved with the film club at university. Any editorial work is useful, like working on the student newspaper or university website. On top of that you need both film and marketing training and the latter can be done part-time while you are doing a postgraduate marketing course.'

Seb is particularly interested in video and Internet technology and appreciates video streaming. 'I am looking forward to the day when most homes have devices where videos can be downloaded. At the moment we rely on television, the pictures and the Internet for our work to be seen,' he says. 'Video on demand is just around the corner and although most consumers will probably be looking for movies to download there will also be room for product demonstrations, sales videos and community videos too. The future is interactive film technology and I am keen to start researching and working on that.'

Seb's day is busy and demanding, with lots of responsibility and interaction with other people. 'I love it, particularly the fact that I have to deal with lots of people all the time.' There are frequent meetings and because this is film-making, there are times when things don't go smoothly and there's lots of waiting around on-set. 'There is always something that needs to be done, though, so I don't get much time to myself,' Seb says.

Skills you'll need

- Seb recommends a good degree with lots of extracurricular interests which involve film, video and marketing. 'The sooner you can start the better,' he says. 'It all helps with the CV.'
- Seb is also interested in film and video technology and he says that it is fairly essential to understand how things work. 'You have to understand the cameras, digital technology and the Internet and, if possible, be able to work with special effects software too.'
- Languages are always useful, but Seb says that he speaks only English and doesn't find it a problem. 'English is the worldwide language for film-makers.'
- Film and video are a method of communicating, but more conventional means are also crucial. 'You have to be able to write a persuasive proposal and a sharp script with good dialogue,' he says. 'Then you have to be able to get the messages across on-screen without the viewer being aware of this.'
- You have to be a team player, because making films involves lots of people, some on-set but most behind the scenes.

Tips

- A good start is simply to watch as many films and videos as possible, including technical productions. There are various books on the theory of film-making, analysing the differences in style between the leading directors. There are many different roles in film-making, from wardrobe to continuity, production to camerawork and lighting. Try to find out which area interests you most.

■ Most schools and colleges have film clubs – join up and practise writing scripts, shooting and editing.

■ Don't forget that films and videos for marketing purposes provide a good living, so find out about marketing as well as films. Learn about the basics of marketing so you understand the objectives of the clients,and how the film media can help them achieve these objectives.

Focus group manager

Money: You'll probably start on £17,000 as a junior, rising to £45,000 after seven years or so, with plenty of perks, like a company car, six weeks' paid holiday and gym membership, which you wouldn't get to start with.

Hours: Some days can be very long, starting at 6 or 7 and finishing at 9 or 10. But there will be other days when there is nothing much going on and you can work from home, perhaps preparing for a group or writing a report.

Health risk: Low from the work itself.

Pressure rating: Medium, but variable. It is stressful when the groups are being organised and run, but there are plenty of quieter moments too. There is also pressure from the clients to make the groups as effective as possible.

Glamour rating: Medium. Market research has never been a topic to set the world on fire, but for those in the industry, the ability to run a good focus group is well respected.

Travel rating: Medium. You may well have to travel to all kinds of areas to get local feedback from consumers and users of a great variety of products or services.

Put ten people together and you come up with 50 different points of view. The purpose of focus groups is to hear from the consumers themselves what they really think about products and brands.

Bernadette Newing worked for a market research agency after leaving university, where she read English and theatre studies. She didn't really expect her theatre studies course to be of such direct benefit, but she has found it invaluable in her focus group work.

'When I was working for the market research company I was asked to arrange a group of 50 computer users and partners to get together to talk about the products and services of one of the agency's clients. The objective was to get away from the marketing hype and all the self-delusion that a room full of marketing professionals can get caught up in. They wanted to get real, to find out what users really thought.'

Bernie organised the group, inviting people from all levels of user, booked the facilities and hosted the event. 'I was briefed by the client so I knew what sort of questions they wanted asked. I acted as the chairperson, raising issues, inviting the users to raise their own issues and getting as much feedback as possible.' She also broke the group into small units for detailed discussions.

Afterwards, Bernie had to prepare a report for the client and other marketing professionals. 'They found it extremely useful. We covered everything from the advertising, the actors they used in the TV ads, the messages and whether they were effective and just general feedback on the marketing and promotion and the product itself. We were able to tell the R&D [research and development] people what the users really thought about the design and function details and they were able to go away and incorporate the suggestions into the next version.'

The exercise was such a success that Bernie now has full responsibility for organising focus groups on all sorts of topics for all kinds of clients. 'Sometimes we use children, other times it's all men or all women or all from a minority group. It depends what the client wants.'

Bernie says she loves the work for several reasons. 'I adore having to work with people in this way. They are doing something unusual and they feel they are being helpful. They are often very keen and enthusiastic and sometimes I even have to moderate what they are saying and cut out the hyperbole. I also really enjoy the three stages of focus group work. First is the planning stage, when I have to work out the questions, the issues, the topics and how the event is going to pan out. Second is the actual event itself and I love running it. I now have an assistant who helps me, which makes it easier for me to focus on the first and third stages. The last stage is the reporting. Sometimes I have to produce a 100-page document full of statistics and summaries. It can be quite technical, because it really is a science as well as an art.'

Out of the focus groups all kinds of decisions are made and strategies planned. Bernie says, 'It is very satisfying because clients will listen to a report from a focus group more readily than from a market research professional who is just giving his advice. It is very rare for the focus group to say anything different to what the market research professional was recommending, but clients listen more readily.' Focus groups can also be useful in deciding which brand name, logo or type of packaging they like.

Bernie says, 'When I did my theatre studies I couldn't really see a use for it apart from my own pleasure, but actually it has proved to be extremely valuable. I know how to have presence in front of a group, how to use my voice to control a situation and how to deal with people. I can also make people relax and have a laugh, which makes the whole thing more entertaining and enjoyable.'

Those in the focus group get paid expenses and a token amount for their time, but Bernie emphasises that it is important not to pay too much or people will say whatever they think you want to hear, in order to be invited again. 'Organising and running focus groups is a very interesting, useful and valuable part of the marketing process,' she says. 'I'm not quite sure how I happened to find the right niche for me, but it suits me very well. I don't even mind the contact with clients or the report-writing. It's all part of the job and it is a job I love.'

Skills you'll need

- Like all marketing professionals, you need first-rate communication and interpersonal skills to run focus groups. Bernie also advises finding someone you respect and asking them how they do it. 'I always look for a mentor when I go into a new job. It helps to learn the most in the shortest time,' she says.

- General marketing experience is almost mandatory, although Bernie says that she studied with the Open University and got some excellent qualifications and experience. 'You can study in your own time with the OU and it suits anyone who is in work but wants more qualifications,' she says.

- The ability to run a meeting is based on some learned techniques, available in any business administration publications. You have to know how to deal with people in the group who dominate and with those who won't say anything. Any group is usually a blend of several personalities and there is a skill in getting the best out of a group and not letting it degenerate into an open, unstructured conversation.

- Any degree which has trained you to think logically and in a methodical way is helpful. You also need to be able to write a succinct report which delivers the information required in the most cogent way. You will also need to present it, often by standing in front of a group of senior managers from the client company, so confidence and a good voice are fairly important.

- Languages are useful, because a growing number of firms want focus groups conducted in advance of their going into foreign countries and expanding their marketing at great expense. French, German, Italian and Spanish are the classic ones, which you will need to business level. Russian is also in growing demand. You'll also need to be aware of the cultural differences when dealing with nationals from these countries – they often have ways of doing things which are strange to us, but you can cause offence and get an inaccurate response if you don't know about their foibles and preferences.

Tips

- If you are a bossy but organised person you'd probably love running a focus group. You need to be able to shepherd other people into smaller groups and get them interested in doing what you want. If your school or university has a theatre group, get involved with that, on the practical side as well as on-stage.
- You need to focus on market research after you've finished university and got some basic marketing qualifications. It is possible to run a focus group without these, but you'll be unlikely to rise above a certain level.
- How about seeking out a market research agency while you are at university and seeing if you can do some part-time work for them? Running focus groups is a major part of market research work and you'll get a good feel for whether you like it or are suited to it. After university, the experience will look good on your CV.

Freelance marketing consultant

Money: £150,000 a year at the top of the profession, although you'll always have the worry that clients will go elsewhere or that your strategies will be wrong. Any perks you'll have to give to yourself.

Hours: Long. You'll never be able to switch fully off and are likely to wake up thinking about clients and campaigns.

Health risk: Low.

Pressure rating: Medium to high. The inability to switch off creates its own stress.

Glamour rating: High. You're likely to work in a high-profile sector.

Travel rating: Medium. Most days will be spent in the office, but you'll also have to meet clients, socialise and network and arrange events. Possibly you'll also need to go to trade shows and conferences, either with clients or to promote yourself.

Marketing professionals usually either work in-house, on their own and with subcontracted third parties or as part of a marketing department, or they work for an agency. But there is a third option, which is to work for yourself. The freelance marketing consultant has his or her own clients and is self-employed.

Francine Rosewall says, 'You don't just leave university with a marketing qualification and then go straight into freelance work. You need to have experience and a reputation and know that work will come and find you before you take the plunge. Even with all those things it can be quite nerve-racking, not knowing where your next job is coming from.'

Francine spent a postgraduate year in the USA at Harvard Business School before coming back to the UK and working for one of the top five marketing agencies. She says, 'I was lucky to have some excellent qualifications before I even started work and then I was lucky to work with some top clients.' She specialised in the beauty and fashion industry and wrote regularly for some of the most prestigious fashion magazines even before she went freelance. 'Once I had decided to go freelance, after eight years, I really had to market myself as much as my clients. I have to always look out for opportunities to build my own brand, which is my name.' Francine has her own column in a magazine for marketing professionals where she gives advice and comments on the industry.

She says, 'Some firms really like to have an independent specialist rather than someone in-house because they can't afford the salary level to get the expertise. They also prefer a sole practitioner to an agency because they feel they are getting better attention and service, which they are.' Francine has a team of other freelancers to back her up and provide specialist skills when she needs them. She says, 'I work with a virtual independent team. We have web designers, copywriters, advertising and market research specialists, a PR planner and a press relations specialist. We work together on projects but rarely meet, doing everything over the Internet, using e-mail and the web.'

Clients get a better quality of service, attention and expertise by using a freelance consultancy, Francine says. 'Agencies often have junior people that they assign to manage clients' accounts, often without the clients being aware of it. And in-house people rarely have the level of expertise and experience that a freelancer can offer. The only problem is that some freelancers take on more work than they really should. But clients often don't know that either.'

Francine arranges all kinds of events as well as marketing strategies for clients. 'I arrange press meetings and launches of new products,' she says. She has an assistant in her office who helps with the practical side, but handles all the press contacts and client meetings herself. 'My job is divided into two parts, really. One is advising clients what they should do and to do that I have to prepare ideas, go to meetings and make recommendations in presentations and reports; and second is the execution of the strategy. Then I have to work with other marketing professionals. I try to use my own contacts but sometimes the clients have incumbents that they want me to work with.'

She says that the ability to get along with anybody is fairly essential. 'It's all about the ability to communicate as well as plan,' she says. 'The actual advice is really easy to give. I have plenty of experience so I know what works and what doesn't. But planning the strategies and seeing them through to the end takes the time.'

She also has to invest in a good wardrobe. 'Most of my clients and the media are working in the fashion and beauty industry and they are really very smartly turned out. So I have to have a good wardrobe with items that I can use for a variety of events and situations.'

The one side of her work that Francine is finding challenging is the use of the Internet. 'I know I have to get to grips with Internet marketing and e-business, but at the moment you could write all I know on the head of a pin.' She is taking evening courses on Internet and e-business software. 'I can use word processing and e-mail, but I really need to know how the Internet can be used in marketing campaigns and what makes a good website,' she says. Luckily, one of her freelance colleagues has that specialist knowledge, and she calls on him when she needs help.

Francine says, 'I love being freelance but its not everyone's cup of tea. You can earn more but there is considerable insecurity. The whole business depends on me. I don't get sick pay or holiday pay; on the other hand I can count a lot of expenses against the business. I like it more for the way of life, being my own boss, than anything else. Although I work for clients I always feel that I can walk away if I don't like them. You can't do that so easily in an agency or when you are in-house. On the other hand, in-house managers never trust an out-of-house person to the same degree as they do internal managers, and you are always struggling for their trust and confidence.' But she says that when they see the results of what she can deliver they start to trust her more. 'The proof of independent marketing is in the strategies and campaigns I devise. I'm not tied down by red tape or protocol – I can cut straight to the chase and just do things.'

Skills you'll need

- Self-confidence by the shed-load on top of plenty of experience and qualifications. You need to be able to sell yourself as well as your client, so self-promotion is essential.
- Languages are also very useful, as most clients are looking to expand into Europe or go global.
- Knowledge of the Internet at a business level – it's not necessary to be technical.

Tips

- Don't think of going freelance until you have several years' in-house or agency experience and know enough people so that you can easily get work. Make this the prime aim of your career plan.

Guerrilla marketer

Money: You'll probably have done several marketing jobs already and found you have a talent for being unusual and innovative and have an unusually creative and innovative approach to marketing scams, so you can command a respectable salary, starting at £25,000 and, depending on your track record, possibly reaching £50,000 or £60,000.

Hours: Unconventional. You're an ideas person and the next big thing could come to you in the bath, at breakfast, on a Sunday walk, whenever. But you'll also have to do routine work such as writing reports and talking to clients in normal business hours.

Health risk: Low. Unless you participate in the more physically outlandish ideas, your job is ideas focused and deskbound. Not much danger there. Just don't fall back on artificial stimulants to kick-start the creative process – that's a one-way street.

Pressure rating: Could be high. The spotlight will be on you to come up with something imaginative, creative, radical and unusual – to order and to a timescale and budget. That's tough, and the chances are that the more pressure is on, the harder it becomes. Having said that, many radical creative people do thrive on stress and pressure.

Glamour rating: High. When you have a great original idea, you are made. Just ensure that no one steals it and everyone knows it came from you.

Travel rating: Medium. You'll have to meet clients and talk to other marketing professionals involved in the campaign, but there will also be a lot of sitting around in meetings and staring at the wall waiting for an idea to come.

No, this doesn't mean you walking down the high street dressed in a gorilla outfit. This is the new face of grab-'em marketing, which snatches headlines and creates news for the manner of the marketing as much as its message. When successful, it's hard to avoid and the impact is high, but get it wrong and it will either sink without trace or create negative headlines for all the worst reasons.

Years of traditional me-too marketing, jaded audiences and bored clients meant the time was ripe for new ways to grab customers' attention. Marketing and PR consultant Simon Davis says, 'Marketers have been forced to resort to scare and shock tactics to catch a potential customer's eye. We call these new

How to get into Marketing and PR

techniques and strategies guerrilla marketing and the people who think up the stunts and promotions and execute them are at the cutting edge of marketing strategies.'

Every guerrilla marketing campaign should be original – the whole point about projecting the image of a naked woman onto the Houses of Parliament, for example, is that no one has done it before. Anyone who imitates it will never achieve the same impact as the first time. Consequently, all guerrilla marketers are constantly trying to think up new schemes, new gags, new campaigns and promotions which will make the headlines and grab people's attention.

Some guerrilla marketing campaigns are dramatic, like dressing up all telephone boxes with red ribbon, while others involve the **adaptation** or sabotage of other people's campaigns. In this post-modern war between the hidden persuaders and consumers who claim that advertising and marketing have no effect on them, marketing takes on new, more subtle, methods. For example, a poster with TV chef Antony Worrall Thompson holding a cup of Nescafé coffee has a speech caption saying 'The only thing I wouldn't change …' A guerrilla marketer has added 'is my underpants', giving the message and his smug look a whole new meaning.

Colin Scott works as a guerrilla marketer for a young dynamic marketing agency. He says, 'A lot of my time is spent sitting around brainstorming. Sometimes we all go out in the hope that the change of surroundings stimulates a new idea and, of course, ideas don't come to order. I seem to have my best ones in the early mornings as I'm waking up and then I have to quickly write them down. Sometimes, by the time I get to the office, the idea is self-evidently rubbish, but every now and then I have a cracker.'

Colin believes that Greenpeace, although not one of his clients, is one of the masters of subversive guerrilla marketing. 'The approach also fits Greenpeace's corporate brand image of being alternative and subversive.' Animal rights campaigners are also expert at subverting other people's advertisements by adding comments in the same colour and typeface so that they look part of the original ad but completely change the meaning. Road protesters removed the 'S' from Shell so that it read 'Hell', and campaigners for the legislation of cannabis changed the familiar Rizla brand so that it read 'Ganja'.

Colin says that thinking up the idea is only part of the job – sometimes the easy part. 'Even once we've got a good idea we have to convince the client. Often they are concerned about the possibility of it going pear-shaped and getting lots of bad publicity. Of course, we want to devise something that is radical, new, never been done before, and even though they've hired us to be radical they have trouble giving us the go-ahead.'

Then, says Colin, the campaign has to be executed. 'Seeing it go live means the most work. First we have to check that what we've got in mind is legal. Often we have to apply for permission and sometimes it is denied and we have to either forget the idea or adapt it. The first idea we have usually gets amended and changed as we go down the line. It may be that the costs are prohibitive, it is too dangerous, illegal or it will cause permanent damage to the environment, or something like that.'

Often the idea needs careful complementary marketing to raise public awareness. 'It's no good just suddenly doing something wild or extravagant out of the blue. The public and the target audience have to be warmed up, teased about it. Sometimes we'll run a **teaser campaign** lasting several weeks, although you have to be careful not to do it for too long or be too obscure or people will either not get it or get fed up with it.'

The consultancy Colin works for has a flat hierarchy and ideas are welcomed from anyone. 'We have a new starter whose job includes collecting and delivering the post around the building making, tea and collecting the sandwich orders. Last week he came up with a brilliant idea at the brainstorming meeting. Now the more senior and experienced ones of us are working out how practical it is, how much it will cost and what supporting marketing and promotion needs to be done. But we've already run it past the client and they think it's brilliant. He'll get a bonus in his next pay packet and probably get promoted once he's got some more general marketing experience.'

Colin says that guerrilla marketers have to understand the nuts and bolts of conventional marketing before they understand what makes a really wild and wacky idea. 'You've got to have something to relate the idea to and understand the psychology of the target audience and what will appeal to them.' He says it is easier to come up with guerrilla marketing ideas for younger audiences. 'They just like to be shocked. You have to be more subtle for the business and **grey markets**.' Guerrilla marketing is a kind of martial art, claims Colin. 'Often what we are doing is turning the energy of a mainstream, politically unacceptable advertiser back against itself, like in judo or ju-jitsu, in our case by changing the meaning of the message. Or we do such dramatic grabbing scams that the campaign is unmissable.'

Guerrilla marketing is often the most complex of all strategies, despite looking easy – it's not just a matter of coming up with off-the-wall ideas. The young man in Colin's office who was responsible for a brilliant idea that might survive to the point where it hits the streets still has to undergo a marketing apprenticeship. 'There is no really fast track,' says Colin. 'Everyone has to pay their dues, although some can do that faster than others.'

Skills you'll need

- Off-the-wall creativity and the ability to think of original high-publicity campaigns that no one else has thought of.
- Lateral thinking. When everyone else is working along textbook lines, you are approaching a problem or issue from another angle, coming up with a solution that is radical and innovative.
- The ability to visualise a solution. High achievers often visualise a solution early on or instantly. This image drives them forward and keeps them going through the time it takes for their colleagues and the client to see their vision.
- A talent for breaking patterns. Take the problem and conventional marketing and promotion techniques and see what happens when you throw in unexpected elements or ideas.
- Strength of character to persuade and convince, but the maturity to walk away from other people's objections or conventional thinking.
- Strong self-belief yet the ability to accept when an idea really is a non-runner. Self-belief is the foundation of creative success.
- Good enough communication skills to help others visualise the solution or idea you have in mind.

Tips

- Practise focusing on your senses – trust your intuition.
- Become a media junkie – follow marketing and promotion campaigns and imagine how you could have done them differently.
- Encourage yourself to be radical – it doesn't matter what other people think.
- Learn to live with put-downs and embarrassments – not all your ideas will work. If one in ten is halfway good, you're doing well.
- When you see a radical, innovative campaign, think what could have gone wrong. Plan how you would have dealt with problems and objections.

■ **Adaptation**

A firm's response to market pressures and other factors whereby it continues to exploit its differential advantage, including looking for new opportunities and responding to threats.

■ **Grey market**

Retired people or people over 50 years old. (Not to be confused with the grey market of illicit unauthorised products.)

■ **Teaser campaign**

A marketing campaign used in advance of a launch or promotion, to intrigue and interest potential customers.

Internet marketing manager

Money: Could be very good. As in any new specialisation, anyone who has more than six months' experience is considered an old hand. And any skill in short supply can demand good money. Starts at £25,000, up to £60,000, but six figures are not unheard of.

Hours: Flexible. The Internet is a **24/7/365** operation and you will be able to structure your working day more or less as you like. However, you'll also have to work with marketing, IT people and clients, who all work more conventional hours.

Health risk: Low. You'll need regular breaks from the screen, shoulder massages and eye tests, but the risk of accident is greater in getting to and from the office.

Pressure rating: Medium to high. Keeping up with advances in both IT and marketing means a degree of multitasking, lots of reading and on-line chat-room discussions.

Glamour rating: Medium to high. As part of the electronic revolution, the Internet marketing manager can probably blind all sides with science.

Travel rating: Low to non-existent. The whole point of Internet marketing is that you communicate through computers and don't have to travel to the office or to client meetings. The occasional trade show, possibly in a glamorous location, is the most you can hope for.

In the information technology age, the Internet is crucially important in all areas of marketing and PR. With it a new job has also emerged, with the focus entirely on delivering marketing concepts, strategies and promotions electronically.

The background for this job could be either conventional marketing or traditional IT, for this is a new type marketing–IT hybrid which requires both skills. The jargon is new, too. For example, Internet marketing firm Broadvision described its relationship with its client Barclays Bank as one based on 'an ongoing commitment to open standards, high performance and scaleability' – terms more familiar to an IT proposal than a marketing brief.

Simon Spicer is an Internet marketing specialist with a PR and marketing agency in central London. He says, 'Marketers have always used database tools and software, but now they are expected to know how to program them and how to use them in an electronic environment. There has also been an explosion in the use of **customer relationship management (CRM)** software tools by marketing departments, and the Internet marketing manager will be expected to know them inside out, not just from the marketing but also from the technological point of view. Even newer are the e-CRM software tools or electronic customer relationship management programs, although as all CRM involves an electronic element these days, the term frankly doesn't mean much. It's just marketing spin by the software companies.'

Simon's background is a hardcore technical one, with a degree in electronic engineering and a first job as a design engineer in a small high-technology design agency, specialising in space technology. He then became a product manager before moving to sales and marketing and then specialising in Internet marketing. He describes how agencies and consultancies are finding themselves competing with IT companies that are also moving into marketing, by offering a vast range of web-connected software for marketing purposes which they claim offers a more personalised, targeted and one-to-one marketing experience. 'Standard marketing companies too have been quick to jump on the Internet bandwagon, but now there is also a new breed of marketing enterprises which are working almost entirely electronically,' he says. 'They have virtual meetings, use webcams and desktop video conferencing and can consequently be based anywhere. The workers can be in Scotland, Cornwall or California and it doesn't matter. And their customers can be anywhere as well.'

Not only do they use IT to run their own businesses, these people also focus on Internet-based marketing strategies and plans. They concentrate on banner and web advertising and know how to develop brands that appeal to particular electronic audiences.

Simon says, 'The Internet marketing manager knows how to use the Internet to get the latest customer profiles, to create more immediate and meaningful reports, advisory documents and proposals. The ability to use the Internet as a tool for research is as important as the ability to use the Internet as a marketing device to reach your customers.'

Some IT and marketing people are uncomfortable with their new proximity. One IBM spokesperson says, 'Marketing ideas have to be implemented much faster than before and that can put a lot of strain on both the specialist marketing people and the technical people who have to implement the campaigns.' The new age of immediacy and interactivity means that every piece of customer communication is part of a work in progress, not the finished article, and this also puts pressure on these managers, adds Simon.

Other marketing professionals like the opportunity to control their plans more directly. After decades of having to refer to the IT people when they wanted something done, they appreciate the chance to get their hands on the software and systems that make it happen. IT is now extremely user friendly and even with a limited level of IT knowledge the Internet marketing manager can still be successful.

The IBM spokesperson continues, 'Software is now available which allows a relatively IT-illiterate marketing manager to create and deliver a sophisticated campaign, monitor it and give feedback on response in a much tighter way than before.'

The new integrated IT and marketing job, in which campaigns are delivered electronically, can also involve other departments such as sales and logistics. Simon says, 'In an average day I find myself talking to managers in many other departments and jobs and having to talk to them about technology and marketing in terms that they understand.'

The problem facing Internet marketers like Simon is how to measure audiences and site hits. All marketers need statistics, need to know reliably whether audience numbers are accurate, what their market share is and what it could be and how innovative their campaign is compared with the competition. There are several agencies that specialise in providing this information, but all have different criteria and methodologies, so often succeed only in throwing up doubts about the value of Internet marketing rather than supporting its efficacy. Simon says, 'The most common technique is using a focus group or panel to give their feedback on the effects of specific web marketing, but this is subjective – there is no sound concrete standard at the moment for site traffic measurement, which means that Internet marketing is a rather inexact science. That is unsatisfactory for everyone.'

Skills you'll need

■ Not either marketing or IT but both. This means a combination that isn't always comfortable or natural – IT techies have a reputation for sometimes lacking in social skills and to be a good marketing person you must have excellent natural social talents. That means you get on with people. Nerdish IT people needn't think about it, but marketing people who like using the web and can program a page or two can make the combination work. Even if you haven't had any training, Internet marketers are famous for picking things up as they go along.

■ Talk to people about their jobs and how much the Internet is affecting what they do. You'll find that there are hardly any jobs today which don't have some element of electronic involvement.

■ Bone up on the cross-over jargon. For example, get used to mentioning 'relationships', 'audience', 'campaigns', 'one-to-one', 'ABC1', 'demographics', 'target marketing' and 'advertising' in the same breath as 'applications', 'security', 'remote access', 'call centres', 'Java', 'scaleability', 'interoperability' and 'open platforms'.

Glossary

■ **24/7/365**
Continuously, 24 hours a day, 7 days a week and 365 days a year.

■ **Customer relationship management (CRM)**
The management of existing customers to ensure their loyalty.

Journalist

Money: Poor. If you want to get rich, don't become a journalist. A staff writer earns £7,000–£10,000. News or features editors can get £15,000, but even the editor of a trade paper is unlikely to earn more than £25,000. If you can't manage on the money you can always cross the fence and become a marketing or PR professional and leave journalism to the young and idealistic.

Hours: Irregular and long. Probably officially 10–6, but press days when the publication closes are usually frantic and you are likely to be expected to work until the magazine or newspaper is put to bed. You'll also have to spend your lunchtimes and evenings entertaining contacts and pundits.

Health risk: Low to medium. As in most office-based jobs the actual risk from injury is limited to electrocution by PC, but the irregular meals and probably high alcohol intake carry their own risks.

Pressure rating: Medium to high. On daily and weekly publications there is always pressure to get an exclusive story or an angle that no one else has spotted or to talk to someone who won't talk to anyone else. There is always a deadline exerting pressure.

Glamour rating: Strangely high. Journalism always seems to attract a combination of scorn and respect. Most people are fascinated by journalists and want to know more about what they do, even though they might profess to distrust them.

Travel rating: Can be good, depending on your seniority on the magazine. When you are junior the most travel you do will be to the printers or production desk, but by the time you get to editor you have to go to press conferences, trade exhibitions and shows, attend seminars and maybe even be a speaker.

Journalism is a career path in itself. Combining journalism with marketing or PR by working for the trade press puts you in a unique position. You will almost be a poacher turned gamekeeper, reporting on people in a very similar sector of the media. Some marketing or PR journalists come from a marketing or PR background, but not many because they'd be taking a drop in salary. But if you really want to be a journalist and are interested in marketing, this is a specialism that has many perks and is great fun.

The most common path into marketing journalism is via postgraduate journalism school. After you've finished your year in college you could be working for any one of the trade titles, such as *Plastic Weekly, Farmers News* or *Computer Dealer*. But luck and determination will get you a job on one of the marketing or PR titles or on the staff of one of the business papers covering the marketing, PR or media sectors.

Steve Slipman, who is a freelancer on one of the marketing weeklies, says, 'It helps to know the marketing and PR world inside out, particularly the firms and people within it, but all the issues too. You'll need to be up to speed with the latest marketing techniques and know who the best spin doctors are and what the most innovative campaigns are like. So a background in marketing as well as journalism is what I'd recommend.'

Like all journalists, you'll always be looking for angles and news. You'll be building contacts within the professional marketing world and keeping a finger on the pulse by developing contacts and using those well known lubricants – food and drink.

Steve says, 'You'll be able to conduct a conversation with the most high-flying marketing professionals, arguing that they are wrong even if you don't believe it. Good journalists can act as Devil's advocate, switching from one side of an argument to another with conviction.'

When you start on a marketing title, you'll probably have to do the editorial assistant's job. This involves opening the post, answering the phone and eventually writing a few stories. You'll probably start on a 'NIB', or news in brief, something mainly written from press releases. Then you'll progress to features, which involve taking an issue, talking to people in the industry and developing both sides of an argument. Features are like essays with a lot more grab and bite, with a beginning, middle and end, and usually with lots of boxes too. These can be a case study illustrating the issue being debated or a list of hints and tips. You'll need to be able to quote people to illustrate points and arguments, so you need interview skills to get people to talk about what you want them to talk about.

On a small title you'll also be responsible for arranging for pictures to be delivered from the PR agency. You might also have to help the subeditor write headlines and check other writers' work. As you progress you'll start to commission freelancers and look for your own news stories.

When you get to editor you'll be playing a lead role in airing some of the industry's sensitive issues, revealing truth and inequality where people want to hide them and campaigning for the abused in the industry. Most trade magazines have a campaigning theme of some sort, defending the livelihood of those in the trade.

Being an editor also means that you have to manage a team of journalists, as well as work with the art editor, the subeditors and the production team and liaise with the publisher and the media sales team. By the time you get to editor you are writing less and managing more and not everyone likes that. Not all good journalists make good editors and you might be happier remaining a staff writer or becoming a freelancer.

'The strange thing about working as a journalist in the marketing and PR world is that while normally the marketing or PR people talk to the press about their client or company, in this scenario they are the focus of your interest,' says Steve. 'If you work for *Computer Dealer* you'd have their PR person along for the ride when you interview a computer dealer – when you work for *PR World*, it is the PR person that you are interviewing.'

Luckily the marketing and PR world is full of interesting characters and risky deals, fascinating campaigns and unscrupulous scams. There are headhunters and ambitious individuals, industry awards, company takeovers, new uses for old technologies, as well as innovative new technologies. It is an exciting, gossipy world with pots of money sloshing around – lots of expense accounts and big salaries. Some of the characters are larger than life and there is always a great deal to write about.

Skills you'll need

■ Writing ability is essential, obviously, but journalism requires a special sort of writing and a good report writer or novelist will not necessarily make a good journalist. The writing skills can be learned, however.

■ You'll need a good memory. There will be plenty of times when you are told something but can't be seen to write it down.

■ You must be able to do research. You shouldn't dream of talking to an interviewee without knowing everything about them. A badly prepared journalist has no credibility.

■ You'll have to be articulate, verbally as well as on paper. A good grasp of English is essential.

■ It helps to have the ability to appear to drink as if you enjoy it. If you prefer Evian or Perrier, that's fine, but be discreet about it.

■ You'll need a thick skin. Not everyone likes journalists and lots of people actively distrust them.

■ You'll learn how to interview people without appearing tactless or pushy. Your subjects will not necessarily want to talk about what you want to talk about or, if they do, they'll want to cast their company in a positive light. You'll have to cut through their agenda to get to yours.

- You'll have to be able to identify a story even if it is being hidden from you. It helps to be cynical.
- The ability to use word-processing software is essential and language skills are useful too. Many marketing and PR people work for global companies and the ability to talk to people in their own language can help you get the inside story.
- You need discipline and dedication.

Tips

- 'I always carry a small notebook and pencil for jotting down things I've been told or overheard,' is the advice that Steve gives.
- Keep a database of contacts, with a secure password. Make notes on their preferences, tastes, hobbies and so forth, so that next time you speak to them, you can be sure to say the right thing.
- Keep a cuttings library on key figures, companies and issues. This will become your own personal library that you can refer back to in future.
- Be a news junkie. Read as much as you can, watch television and listen to the radio. Your subjects will be using the media to get their clients' message across, so you need to know what the trends and issues are.
- Never reveal your sources. Developing a career as a journalist depends on your sources being able to trust you. You should be prepared to go to prison before revealing a source.
- You are representing your reader, listener or viewer. So always put their point of view to get the answers they'll be interested in hearing.
- Most publications depend on advertising for revenue, but never get too friendly with those responsible for placing advertisements – they'll want you to mention them in the editorial in a positive light.
- Negotiate a good expense account for entertaining informants and gossips, analysts and pundits. If you don't, you'll depend on the PR or their client to pay, and that can leave you indebted to them – not a comfortable position for a journalist to be in.

How to get into Marketing and PR

Lawyer

Money: Good to excellent. You may be on a salary, which can start at around £25,000, or be a freelancer on a retainer. You'll have to make sure that you keep a record of the time you spend with each client and that the billings to each cover your time. Income can easily reach six figures and if you become a barrister with a specialisation in media issues, the sky is the limit.

Hours: Regular at the beginning, but always quite long. Often starting at 9 and finishing at 6. If you have to research or prepare for a case, you could be working late into the night. But the rewards can be rich. The only lawyers who ride bicycles do so by choice.

Health risk: Low. There will be a few Rottweilers in court, but if you are any good you can give as good as you get.

Pressure rating: Medium to high. Particularly if you advise a client badly or miss a trick in the small print of a contract. Then the buck stops with you.

Glamour rating: Medium. In the marketing industry, the legal role is not seen as being high on the glamour list. A shame really, because it is probably one of the most interesting.

Travel rating: Low. Apart from going to local courts, the chances of travel are slight until you become a senior lawyer. Then you'll have to travel the world to advise clients, help with negotiations and ensure that contracts are in your clients' interests.

Once you become a lawyer you can specialise in media law, a fascinating branch of the legal profession. But you'll have to do your apprenticeship and study all aspects of law first, pass your solicitor's exams and practise general work for a few years before specialising in the media, and marketing and PR in particular. Few lawyers started as marketing or PR professionals before becoming media law specialists, but plenty of qualified lawyers want to specialise in media issues because the people and subjects are so interesting. Unlike many of his or her colleagues, a media lawyer will be involved in a fast-moving, hi-tech and glamorous world, a million miles from usual legal fare such as conveyancing.

Unlike many branches of the law, a media specialisation can take you into all sorts of fascinating areas. Mainly, you'll have to be familiar with the rulings and precedents covering plagiarism, libel and slander, as well as contract law. David Spicer is a partner in a law firm with a department specialising in marketing and media law. He says, 'You'll need to do the full formal legal training including articles, but you can have your eye on a career in marketing law from an early stage. The earlier you decide, the more you can specialise throughout your training, even though you'll have to include all other topics as well in the early stages of training.'

As a qualified lawyer, you'll probably be retained by an agency or the marketing or PR department of a big corporate and you'll be asked to check campaigns before they start to run. For example, some bright spark might have devised a campaign which mentions competing products in a detrimental light, or a competitor might be doing the same as regards your client or company. You'll have to know exactly how far they can go without infringing the legal rights of others. Your job will be to launch a legal attack through the courts if your competitors go too far, and to advise your own side on how far they can go.

To do this you'll have to understand the laws that protect brands and images, and the laws of patent. When the marketing professionals develop a new product you'll have to check that no one else has already taken the name or image and know how far the laws of 'look and feel' will allow some overlap. Once journalists start to write about the product or service, you'll have to check what they are saying and ensure that their criticism is fair. You'll have to make sure that the trademark is registered and then set about protecting it if anyone else tries to use it without permission.

David says, 'Marketing and PR professionals obviously have to operate within the law and there are many restrictions that they can infringe without being aware of it. So, as the company or agency lawyer, you should be checking all the campaigns and publicity material before it is released and making sure that the contracts between employers and employees, clients and suppliers and customers are legal. You have to know how far a company can go in its claims and be aware of the consumer protection legislation which protects customers from being sold something that fails to work or meet the promises of the marketers.'

You might also have to advise a firm if a customer is injured, physically or emotionally, by a product that they are selling. If the firm is sued for damages, you will be responsible for putting together a defence case and possibly launching counter-litigation. This can be an aggressive move intended to intimidate the other party, but there is always a possibility that you will end up in court, defending your company or client and/or claiming damages against another. Sometimes you will have to brief a barrister, who may also be a media specialist, or you may act for yourself and present your own case to the court.

The sums involved in media law settlements can be quite stupendous. It is not uncommon for someone injured by a product to be awarded millions in damages, especially if punitive damages are involved, making an example of an individual or a firm.

David says, 'A big part of your work will be on Internet and electronic business law and the laws covering cyberspace use and marketing in cyberspace. These are quite unique and cross international boundaries. For example, the Data Protection Act in the UK is quite different from the Protection of Data and Freedom of the Individual laws in the USA. Data collected in the UK might be illegal in the USA, and vice versa. So you have to not only know about UK media law but also international rulings and restrictions.'

You'll have to negotiate contracts and deals for your company or client with suppliers or other agencies. Agreements with printers and subcontractors, for example, all have to be ratified with individual responsibilities, liabilities and restrictions made very clear. You'll become a dab hand at reading other lawyers' contracts and spotting a phrase or clause that could have a big impact on your firm.

You'll also have to know employment law, for marketing professionals are often restricted from talking about their old employers or taking clients with them if they start up their own agency, for example. You might have to take action on behalf of a client who finds that someone else is using their trademark, a trade name or company name as a **domain name**. David says, 'You'd start by negotiating with the miscreants on behalf of your client or proceed directly to court.' As the lawyer, you'd know all about the dispute resolution procedures for resolving arguments about trade name and domain name clashes.

There are also laws covering the use of mailing lists, which are different in the UK and mainland Europe, and the laws of sale and contract to consumers. It will be your responsibility to make sure that the company you are working for doesn't get into any legal trouble and, if it does, to deal with it. David says, 'It is challenging working in a sector without frontiers but within a legal framework on territorial terms.'

Although the media lawyer's work is heavily involved with textbooks and theories, laws and precedents, contracts and agreements, there is also plenty of time to mix with the creative types and meet glamorous clients. David says, 'Increasing numbers of Internet firms have a lawyer in-house.'

A legal training will always stand you in good stead and even if you don't practise as a lawyer in the media industry, you can move into any other specialist marketing role. Many managing directors, CEOs and captains of industry have legal training as their background. The skills of debate and negotiation and the ability to argue a position will make you a strong candidate for any senior marketing position and might even get you onto the board. For a lawyer, the appeal of working in the new media is that you'll be working alongside bright individuals who are highly motivated to achieve and succeed. David says, 'The culture is entrepreneurial, dynamic and meritocratic. People work very hard but there is a refreshing sense of working together to build a new company, a new industry and a new economy.'

Lawyers working for Internet marketing businesses comes from a variety of legal specialisms, mostly IT but also intellectual property, commercial, mergers and acquisitions, corporate finance and securities law. David says, 'There are only a handful of established "Internet lawyers" although the number is growing fast and there is only a limited amount of "Internet law". Often it is a matter of applying existing law by analogy to the new issues that the Internet presents and finding legally compliant ways of achieving the business objectives. However, an increasing amount of Internet-specific legislation is in the pipeline.'

Contrary to a widely held view, many Internet marketing companies have seasoned professionals at the helm who are building businesses to last. David says, 'Longevity requires firm foundations and it means that lawyers have an opportunity to make a major impact and, of course, to reap significant rewards.'

Skills you'll need

- After A levels you'll go to university to take a law degree and then spend at least two years in 'articles' or contracted to a solicitor or law firm as a junior to learn the practical ropes before your final exams. Even then, you'll have to start at the bottom, doing much of the donkey work. So you must be prepared for some hard work.
- Gift of the gab. You'll have to articulate arguments in a logical way, grasp technical and dry subjects and debate them with others who are trained to do so.
- You have to be able to grasp the detail of any argument in a short time. So the ability to speed-read and absorb the nub of a matter is essential.
- You'll have to have a good memory to be able to recall all those laws and precedents, as well as details of historic contracts and agreements which affect your client or company.
- You'll have to deal with clients, but the ability to get along with people is not as essential as it is in other marketing

jobs. In fact, provided you know your job as a lawyer and can be relied on to keep a company out of trouble, your interpersonal skills are almost irrelevant. Not quite, but almost. Your intelligence and ability to argue and negotiate will be rated far more highly than your ability to charm.

■ You need the ability to keep lots of balls in the air, juggling issues and points and trying to arrive at a final contract which is legal, satisfies everyone, but is slightly in your clients' favour. Remember that the others involved in the negotiations will also have a lawyer trying to do the same thing.

■ Watch *Kavanagh QC* and reruns of *Perry Mason*. See how they act on behalf of their client no matter what their personal feelings? That's a vital skill.

■ Read the trade press and watch out for examples of litigation. When a company gets sued for brand infringement, consider what you would have done.

Glossary

■ **Domain name**
A registered website address. At one time these were limited to a few suffixes, such as .co.uk, .org or .com, but these days the potential is almost unlimited. In the early days of the Internet a few individuals registered names of famous people and companies and then sold them the rights to the domain name at exorbitant rates, but this practice has now been made illegal.

List manager

Money: Low to medium, starting at around £12,000 and peaking at around £18,000. The career path is restricted and perks are very limited. If you go on to launch your own list rental business you could make far more, but starting and running a business involves a lot more than simply being a list manager.

Hours: Regular. Probably 9.30–5.30, without much need for overtime.

Health risk: Low. If you encounter a virus it will probably be of the computer variety.

Pressure rating: Low. Only gets high if you make a mistake and ten samples or free gifts get sent to the same journalist.

Glamour rating: Low. It is not a high-profile job, even if the clients using the lists are.

Travel rating: Low. You'll work regular hours and rarely leave the office building.

Not a high-profile or glamorous job but essential when the marketing professionals are considering a direct mail campaign. These days the job is highly technical and you'll have to understand the latest database and market research technology. Can be a temporary or permanent step sideways for an account manager seeking more experience in direct marketing. Every direct marketing professional should know what a list manager does.

The list manager is responsible for keep the mailing lists 'clean' and up to date, which means making sure that there are no duplications, outdated entries or gaps. Sometimes an entry can get confused by elements being rekeyed several times, perhaps the same person's surname spelled slightly differently each time or with a slight difference in the address, but it is up to the list manager either to trawl a list manually or conduct searches on the database to pick up these sneaky duplicates.

You need to understand the technology, both at a superficial 'what it does' level and a technical 'how it does it' level. You'll have to understand database programming techniques and languages like 4GLs and know the main database languages such as Oracle and Informix.

Sarah Powell has been a list manager with a large marketing agency for four years and she says, 'The work can be routine but it can be fascinating. You have to be exact and thorough and I did a year's course working on databases and database programming as well as a specialist course on direct marketing.'

Lists are mainly used by direct marketers, so there will be contact with direct marketing managers as well as general marketing managers. Lists can be of existing customers as well as potential customers, which can be pulled from lists that you have bought or traded. By developing and maintaining up to date lists of customers, which include name and address but also many details such as recent purchases, lifestyle, job and family status, a company can greatly improve the effectiveness of its marketing campaign. By canny use of a list the company can target its marketing. With today's technology a list can, in theory, comprise a single customer, depending on the criteria set.

A clean database can be used for marketing research, categorising according to frequency of purchase and type of purchase. There are many other ways to sort a list, perhaps according to season of purchase, time of day of purchase or by considering other products purchased at the same time. A good list can help a company target promotions to specific users, either electronically or by direct mail.

Lists are frequently enormous. One tobacco company has a list with 50 million names on it, for example, and that is not unusual. The list manager will be responsible for sourcing and negotiating new lists and integrating them with existing lists so that there are no duplications. This can be awkward if the two lists were originally created with different formats, but these days nothing is impossible.

Sarah says, 'I work with the research team and help them develop a marketing strategy and then execute it. I am responsible for continually refreshing the list and looking for new ways to source data. It is an interesting job but it needs a picky mind that likes things well organised, as well as the ability to negotiate deals on list sales and purchases.'

Sarah did most of her training with a specialist list rental agency, but now works for a large marketing agency in charge of all their lists for all their clients. She says, 'It's a bit of a back-room job that would suit someone who doesn't want to meet the clients too often, if at all. Programming and database skills are probably more important that marketing skills. Basically, I do what the marketing manager tells me to do and extract lists from the databases that we hold according to criteria that other people define. But I enjoy it. It's very logical and relaxing work.'

Skills you'll need

■ An understanding of the law, particularly regulations protecting the individual against intrusion.

- Sarah says, 'An obsession with accuracy and detail is essential and it helps if you are a pedant. You've got to have a good eye for detail.'
- A creative mind helps when it comes to new ways to divide and expand an existing list.
- Technical ability, with an in-depth understanding of database and programming technology. Also a knowledge of data storage and retrieval technology and an understanding of the Internet and how it can be used for list management and use.
- The ability to negotiate with customers and vendors of lists. You'll need to be able to see the potential value of lists, and know how to spot a list that it is not all it is cracked up to be.

Tips

- Start making lists now. Then redefine your lists according to different topics. If this excites you, this could be the career for you.
- Study logic and programming – both are useful for list managers.
- This is the sort of job that is often recruited internally, so get yourself a position in a marketing consultancy or department that you really want to work for doing anything, and then keep your eyes and ears open. Start in the post room – the staff who collect and deliver the post get to see everyone within the organisation and are often the first to hear about career vacancies.

Marcoms manager

Money: Varies. As a marcoms assistant you could start on £12,000 rising to £17,000 before you get a job as a junior marcoms manager. Then your salary could reach £22,000 before you get the full marcoms manager job title. It could rise through promotion to £50,000 or £60,000, if you are in charge of the marcoms department with a team of marketing and PR people working for you.

Hours: Unlikely to be regular or short. This is a busy job which will be pulling you in lots of directions. There will always be something to do and often a panic or crisis over one thing or another.

Health risk: Low to medium. You'll be racing around trying to do lots of jobs at once, so you'll be more accident prone than someone with a more sedate job.

Pressure rating: High. Not only do you have a lot of jobs to do, you'll have responsibility for the execution and results.

Glamour rating: Depends on the company you're working for. If you start with a small company as a jack of all marketing trades and stick with it as it grows, you could find yourself the star of a rising company. By the same token, you might just be exploited mercilessly.

Travel rating: Medium. Even if you spend a lot of time in the building, the chances are that you'll be forever in different offices and departments. As for the wider world, you'll have to organise exhibitions at trade shows and press events, so some travel is possible, but it's doubtful whether it will be particularly glamorous. Contrariwise, part of the job will be to meet and entertain journalists, so trips to fashionable restaurants and watering holes might be on the cards.

This is a combined marketing and communications role. It is mainly marketing, with an emphasis on PR, the communications element being that you have to 'sell' stories to the press and convey a good impression of your company or client. The term is often used in small or medium firms where there isn't enough work to justify two people doing marketing and media communications separately.

Marcoms job specifications can vary considerably between employers and in some firms the communications aspect can mean promoting the firm through all channels, not just the media. In other firms communications can mean press relations, in some customer relations. But it is invariably a combination of two or more jobs with the objective of raising the profile of the company and its products and services among consumers and the press.

Jane Dillsbury is marcoms manager for a small specialist IT modem manufacturer and supplier based in Berkshire. She says, 'The firm I work for is small with only 50 employees, so the marketing and publicity role has been brought under one umbrella. It means that there is always lots to do and I have to be a self-starter and self-motivated, but the beauty of it is that I am virtually my own boss and can do what I like.'

Jane has to devise her own marketing and publicity campaigns and deal with the specialist agencies that the firm uses for advertising, copywriting, printing, poster publicity and point-of-sale marketing. She says, 'I need to be well organised, but being virtually my own boss means that I can walk into any department in the company and talk to managers as an equal. They all want publicity, because they know that it benefits the sales figures.'

Jane has to do all the marketing jobs, including dealing with the press and writing releases and arranging interviews with the trade and national press. She says, 'Sometimes I feel overworked because the press and PR work alone is probably a full-time job. On top of that I have to work with the product managers to talk about branding and pricing and promotion and channel and reseller publicity. I've just taken on an assistant to help me with the Internet marketing and to create a website that can be used for sales transactions, but I know some marcoms managers who have to manage the website too.'

Many marcoms managers complain that they are overworked and overstretched. The fact that many agencies and large marketing departments split the marketing role into many components, like campaign administrator and pricing or promotion manager, indicates that each task can be a full-time one. Freelance and independent marketing people also act as marcoms managers, often doing all the marketing jobs themselves. It can be challenging for those who like to be busy but are organised and efficient. Jane says, 'I come in every morning and have to check through about five or six completely different tasks and chase people doing completely different functions. Sometimes I'm following up on e-mails for half an hour or writing reports or strategy briefings, booking advertising space or talking to journalists. I love it, but I can imagine that some people would find it too much.'

Often, the job involves supervising third parties to whom various tasks like advertising and sales promotion are subcontracted. Sometimes it involves sales development too, and in some cases the marcoms person comes from a sales background. If so, they'll probably know lots about the product but less about the theory and practice of marketing.

The marcoms manager has plenty of variety, then, and a job as a marcoms assistant is a very good way of getting an all-round grounding in the marketing function and how it connects with other departments. Jane says, 'When I started I had no idea about IT or modems and I had to learn about that and the products over the first few weeks. I still don't quite understand how they work, but that doesn't matter. Provided I understand the target customers and can think of new ways to reach them and interest them and persuade them to buy, then I'm doing my job.'

Skills you'll need

- Jane says, 'You've got to be a well-organised person, there's no doubt about that. An interest in marketing is more important than an interest in the products or services, although it obviously helps if you know something about them in advance.'
- She also recommends starting as a marcoms assistant in a large company where you can learn from the more experienced marcoms and specialist marketing consultants.
- A levels and a degree are probably essential, although the subject is less important. Jane says, 'A degree gave me the ability to be structured and organised and also analytical about the material that I have to read and absorb. You have to be able to multitask when you are a marcoms manager.'
- A foreign language or two is helpful, as is the ability to run meetings.

Tips

- When you are at university make sure you join the debating club to hone your negotiating skills, as well as sports and social groups, and be as active as possible. Get onto the organising committees and do as much as you can in the publicity and marketing of these groups. If you can do all this and come out with a decent degree too, you'll make a good marcoms manager.

Market researcher

Money: Starting as a junior or assistant, even with a degree, can mean low pay for a while, such as £12,000 or £15,000, but it can rise quickly to £18,000 or £20,000. As you gain more experience, meeting clients and creating analysis and reports, your worth will rise and you can start to demand more. At the top end, a skilled, experienced market researcher can earn £80,000 to £100,000, plus many perks such as company car, gym membership, healthcare, long holidays and more.

Hours: Starting regular but becoming longer as you progress. Even as a junior, it will help if you don't mind staying late to help produce reports, analyse data and prepare questionnaires.

Health risk: Low. There is plenty of variety in this job, but not much risk to health.

Pressure rating: Medium to high. There is always a need for accuracy, with serious ramifications if you make mistakes. As you become more senior and have to deal with clients, the pressure rises along with the salary.

Glamour rating: Low to medium. This is often perceived as a back-room job. It is the nuts and bolts on which the more glamorous sides of marketing are based.

Travel rating: Medium to high. Senior market research consultants can find themselves jetting all over the country, Europe or the globe. Depending on the type of research and the client, there can be plenty of travel to meetings or to arrange surveys.

No marketing decision should be taken without research. Despite claims that 'clients use research as a drunk uses a lamp post – more for support than illumination', the marketing professional needs information and analysis about market demand, customers, competition, dealers and other forces in the marketplace before they can plan their marketing strategies. Tod Nailor, a consultant market researcher, says, 'To manage a business well is to manage its future. And to manage its future is to manage information.' So information, created through market research, is not just essential for making better business decisions but is also a marketing asset which can give a company competitive advantage.

A market researcher needs a combination of a keen, analytical mind and the ability to communicate easily and well so that they can report verbally and in writing to the managers who need the information. Tod says, 'The job of market researcher is a cerebral one also requiring good interpersonal skills.' He explains that the job involves many meetings with the marketing, product and brand managers, to assess their information needs. 'Then I develop and extract the information from a variety of sources and with a mixture of means and finally distribute the conclusions and results back to the managers who need it.' This demands the ability to write well, in a logical, clear way.

The market researcher has to establish the best source or combination of sources of information to arrive at the answers to the questions being posed. It may be 'vox pop' or voice-of-the-people interviews conducted with people in the street, controlled think-tanks or focus group meetings. Sometimes the information comes from internal sources, such as sales records, sometimes through marketing intelligence and other forms of research. Tod says, 'It is a very logical process and involves introducing logic and reason to random records and reports.

'Data can be secondary or primary – that is, some of it will have been gathered in the course of another activity like sales, while some will be gathered specifically for research purposes.' Frequently, the answers to questions come from existing data, and part of the market researcher's job is tracking down and identifying the right data source and the appropriate route to extract it.

Some information will be qualitative, measuring a small sample of customers' views, and some will be quantitative, based on statistics from a large number of consumers. Tod says, 'Sometimes we decide to undertake observational research by gathering primary data and observing real people, actions and situations. For example, we were working for a food products manufacturer and sent researchers into supermarkets to find out the prices of competing brands or how much shelf space and display support retailers give our client's products.'

Sometimes Tod commissions a telephone survey. 'We find that is best for gathering descriptive information,' he says. He often uses agencies to undertake the actual research, but it is Tod and his team who devise the questions and analyse the results.

'Sometimes we choose to do experimental research,' he says. 'Then we select matched groups of subjects and give them different treatments, controlling unrelated factors and checking for differences between the groups. Thus experimental research can explain the cause and effect relationships between products and customers.' For example, Tod commissioned research for a well-known megastore to establish whether stocking a new product from a famous perfume manufacturer would expand the store's customers and sales in other departments. 'We were also able to establish acceptable pricing levels and strategies,' he says.

Getting the questions right is part of the skill. For example, it will be no good asking children 'What do you think of this product?'; it's better to ask them 'If you were to tell your friend about this, what would you say?' The same applies to questions to any group of consumers or business people. Age, gender, location and income are all factors which affect how questions are phrased to get the quality of results necessary. Interpretation of results is crucial and what sets a novice apart from an experienced market researcher is the ability to see the implications of a set of data or results. Tod says, 'Market research companies and individual consultants place great importance on their ability to translate information into practical recommendations. Knowledge of consumers' attitudes and skills in applying as well as collecting research data is fiercely defended as their own territory.' Some agencies, for example, have their own methodologies and paradigms, such as the Nielson techniques for defining customers according to job type and income or those of the NOP Research Group, which runs opinion polls.

Increasingly, the Internet is being used to get consumers to reveal valuable data and to conduct surveys. The advantage is that distance is no object and the surveys can be well targeted. However, there is no real control over the accuracy of the answers given and therefore some Internet-based research can be fundamentally flawed. Many market research agencies have consultants or whole departments dedicated to developing electronic research. Tod says, 'On-line data collection makes a lot of sense and it is interesting how these techniques are being developed to encourage high-quality responses.' However, on-line research should be only part of an overall strategy. 'There are many additional benefits to a face-to-face approach that go beyond simple number-crunching.'

Tod adds, 'Good researchers are like truffle hounds. They love to hunt for solutions, but they need the time and freedom to explore all the possible ways to get to the end result.' Often he has to face tough problems, he says, 'and they don't have simple solutions.' This is also why good market research can cost a lot of money. 'Good advice is in demand so can be expensive, but it can be priceless,' says Tod. 'When people pay a lot for it, they expect something that they can rely on and which has true value in helping them come to good business decisions.'

There are frustrations in being a market researcher. Sometimes the marketing professionals only see the research results they want to see or they use it too late in the planning process simply to reinforce what they think they already know. Anita Roddick of the Body Shop says that, for many marketers, 'research is no more than a glimpse in the rearview mirror'. Tod adds that it is more like 'turning on the headlights' so that the right way forward for the business can be clearly seen. He goes on, 'The trouble with marketing is that only 50 per cent of it works – the trick is knowing which 50 per cent. Market research can help spot which 50 per cent is going to work and make it deliver more results than the other 50 per cent.'

You'll need to be able to handle clients, who can often be extremely exacting, if not downright difficult. But Tod says, 'These days market research is an accepted part of the marketing process, so there is less struggle required to impress on the client that it is necessary.' Nevertheless, you'll need the judgment to know who you can approach and how often and how much of what they say you can use and attribute. Tod explains, 'You want every interviewee to come away from an interview feeling positively disposed towards the interviewer and the client.'

Skills you'll need

- 'We have to work closely with all executives within the marketing department and the organisation,' says Tod. 'The successful market researcher needs a combination of skills including maths and statistics, as well as English and IT.' People skills are crucial, combined with analytical and interpretative ability to express the results. Tod adds, 'You have to enjoy being in meetings, being able to express yourself in meetings, and get along with clients and colleagues. Although this is a head-down job there are still plenty of times when it is all about reports, liaison and negotiations.' Many groups you will want to research, such as politicians, the media and the FTSE top 250 companies, will be difficult – trained and media wary. So you'll need skills of diplomacy and charm to maintain goodwill so that you can use people again and again.
- You'll need to be objective and not allow your personal tastes and opinions to influence reports or results. Conversely, though, your personal interpretation will sometimes be required, so you'll need to be someone who has views and can express them.
- This is a job that suits someone who likes a challenge, who likes order and processes and enjoys meeting and working with people. 'It really is a people job,' says Tod, 'but you also have to know how to use computer software and know statistics and logic.'

- Languages are also useful in market research, particularly when working for companies that are considering expanding into a European market. Margaret Crane, who runs a pan-European and UK-based market research organisation, says, 'We work for clients across Europe. One day I'm in Paris, then London, then Brussels.' She also has to organise teams of interviewers to conduct the research that she has planned and to use the questionnaires she constructs. 'It is a job with lots of variety and can be full of surprises. You never know what the research will find.'

Tips

- Tod says that anyone interested in science and maths would probably like a career in market research. 'Start looking out for market research and you'll soon realise that many stories in the newspapers are based on a statistic or a fact. Every day there are at least two or three in every newspaper. These almost always come from market research and you can start to see how it affects business decisions.'
- To be a good market researcher you have to be confident enough to ask strangers questions about their habits and tastes – start by conducting such research among your family and friends.
- Make a habit of doing puzzles and solving problems. Anything which stretches your mind will be good practice for being a market researcher.
- Reply to all the surveys you can. Become adept at knowing the structure of questionnaires – and try to work out what the researchers are trying to achieve by asking certain questions.

Marketing assistant

Money: Low. Could be as bad as £8,000 a year, but if you prove yourself could rise to £15,000 before you are in line for promotion to marketing executive or even marketing manager. Not many perks, except perhaps the occasional sample product.

Hours: Standard 9–5 or 10–6. You won't be expected to work overtime, but offering to do so will help your reputation.

Health risk: Low. Travelling to work is probably more dangerous than being there.

Pressure rating: Low. If you find it stressful at marketing assistant level, its probably not the right career for you.

Glamour rating: If you've made a good choice and work for the marketing department of a record company, the glamour rate is high. But if you work for a fridge-maker, no one is going to be very impressed.

Travel rating: Low. The most adventurous trip will probably be to the post office to get the franking machine updated or to the printers to pick up some posters.

This is the first step in marketing. You may be a graduate or you may have come from another industry or even straight from school, but you'll have to be submissive and observe, learn and be prepared to do anything. Some marketing assistants work for in-house marketing departments, others for agencies. They can be very young and start at 17 or, more usually, as graduates at 22. They are frequently regarded as the office dogsbody. But if you are conscientious and reliable, it is a quick stepping stone to another more interesting job with more responsibilities.

If you know you want a career in marketing you have two choices – go to university or college and do an English, media studies or marketing course, or directly approach a firm you'd like to work for and ask if they have a junior vacancy in their marketing department. They will probably be impressed with your initiative and give you a chance, but you must be prepared to do almost anything.

Many marketing directors expect even their most junior assistants to be graduates with degrees, however.

A job as a marketing assistant is a good way to have a go at all the roles in the marketing department. One day you might be working with the art or advertising team, another day with the direct sales marketing and promotion executives.

Lindsay Brown, who has been in marketing for over 20 years, says, 'The marketing assistant's job is to help out everyone else. They won't have much serious responsibility, yet everything they do will be important to those around them. They must take it seriously.'You'll probably find that most of the tasks you are given are checked to make sure you've done it right. If the level of supervision starts to drop, take that as a compliment – it means you are doing things right and they feel less need to watch over everything you do. But if they don't ease back on the double-checking, don't be insulted. Those who delegate to you have responsibility for what you do and they have to check.

The actual tasks and levels of responsibility given to the marketing assistant vary enormously with the type and size of organisation, according to Lindsay.'You are there to be cheerful and available, willing to help the more senior marketing executives, managers and the director, when they have more to do than they can cope with. Mainly, it will be general administrative and practical tasks and basic marketing jobs. But this is how and where you learn, so keep your eyes and ears open. Keep reading marketing theory books and try and work out how the practical tasks you are doing fit into the classical marketing techniques.'

Zara Gibbs, who has been a marketing assistant for six months, says,'You will undoubtedly be asked to make tea and coffee. You will also probably be asked to track press cuttings, cut them out and mount them and send them to clients, perhaps on a daily basis. You might have to set up meetings, making sure that everyone knows that their attendance is required and keep notes during the meetings, which you have to write up and distribute afterwards.' Other jobs that Zara has had to do include photocopying, scanning, keeping media lists up to date, booking travel for clients and colleagues, organising food and coffee for meetings and calling magazines for forward feature lists. In addition, she says,'You might easily be responsible for opening the post, collating reports, delivering memos, writing letters, chasing overdue items and so on. You might have to check the e-mails, sort out the incoming faxes and make sure outgoing faxes are sent. You might have to "clean" the mailing lists by ringing round and checking that the recipients are still alive and interested. You might have to do basic data entry, keying information or text into a PC. All very basic but absolutely essential to the smooth running of the department.'

Some marketing assistants will have degrees in specialist areas, such as journalism and media skills, and will be expected already to be competent in those areas. But all marketing assistants will be expected to think and act like trainees, gratefully picking up skills and tips for the future. Gradually, the jobs that the assistant does will be more and more 'real' and an important part of the overall campaign.

Often the first job given to a marketing assistant is connected with market research. You'll have to use libraries and the Internet to check products and markets or go down to the street and conduct a vox pop. You'll create questionnaires to extract appropriate information and knowledge that can be used to create the right campaign. You'll help build a customer profile that will be used in the campaign development and in defining the objectives. You may start to take production responsibility, ensuring that things happen on time according to the project milestones. You'll have to start liaising with third parties, like printers, and developing your own relationships with the people there.

If there is an exhibition you'll probably be expected to help man the stand. This is a tiring and stressful job, often lasting several days. You just have to pass out literature, encourage people into the stand and answer questions as best you can. The point is to impress potential customers and spread information, and at exhibitions a lot comes down to your charm and interpersonal skills. There may also be promotional events that you have to take part in, although with luck you won't have to dress up in a silly costume. Don't be surprised if you do, however.

Many organisations take their responsibilities towards their marketing assistants very seriously and will send them on courses and training schemes whenever possible and appropriate, and allow them to sit in with planning and client meetings so that they can learn. If this happens, it is best to keep quiet and just observe. It is also not unusual to have marketing assistants assigned to senior executives, managers or directors, acting as personal assistants and expected to watch and learn how the job is done.

After eight or 12 months as a marketing assistant you'll probably have a good idea of which aspect of marketing interests you most. You can start to think about specialising, although you should expect to stay in the assistant job for at least a year. No one likes it when they spend weeks training up an assistant only to have them leave within the next few weeks. While nobody expects you to stay for ever, a year is about average and looks acceptable on your CV.

It might even be three or four years before you get promoted to executive and sometimes it is necessary to move companies to get the promotion you want. This is accepted within the marketing industry and put down as 'gaining experience', provided you do not hop too often between employers. That looks suspicious and prospective employers will question why you haven't stuck at one job for long. So aim for at least a year in each position, possibly two.

Skills you'll need

- You'll need basic computer skills and good handwriting and to be bright and keen. Intelligence and enthusiasm count for more at this stage than formal skills. However, you should have the basic IT and interpersonal skills which show that you will be able to progress and learn.
- You'll have to be able to deal with the public in a charming and competent way, although there will be people around to help you and give you the scripts you need.
- You'll need to be outgoing and confident, although not over-confident or brash. You have to be sensitive to the politics of the office and the relationship between the department and other departments or the consultancy and the client.
- You'll need to be discreet and able to keep secrets – most marketing campaigns have a phase when everything needs to be kept under wraps. Sometimes you'll need tact and discretion when handling different directors or different product managers – each one will expect their needs to take priority.

Tips

- Never say no to whatever task you are asked to do – however lowly, it is a chance to learn more about the marketing process. Nothing must be too menial for you.
- Never gossip – you'll find that marketing departments are often hotbeds of office tittle-tattle and intrigue, but you'll be more popular and get further if you never repeat anything that's said to you, or comment on others in the team.
- Fit in and dress like the rest of the office. This is not a place to try out your holiday outfit. If in doubt, dress modestly and seriously.
- Flirting with senior executives may be fun but won't help your career prospects.
- Be conscientious about time-keeping. Senior managers make their first judgments on simple things like whether you are at your desk on time every day.
- Avoid long personal phone calls. Marketing departments are often relaxed places in which to work, but don't think that people don't notice if you make long-distance calls or your friends call you every day.
- If you have a deadline for a task you've been set, make sure you meet it. If you don't think you are going to, tell someone before the deadline has passed.

How to get into Marketing and PR

Marketing director / Head of marketing

Money: This is the top of the tree, so you can expect at least £40,000 a year and probably nearer £100,000. The perks are extensive, from company car to lots of travel, private healthcare and gym membership.

Hours: You need to be flexible. By the time you get to director you have serious levels of responsibility and regular hours are for the junior staff. However, if you are good at managing the department you can get the executives and managers to stay late while you network on the golf course – just as important as finishing a report.

Health risk: You could get a golf club in the eye, get tangled up in a fishing hook or get injured on some other corporate hospitality event, but the only health risk in the office is being stabbed in the back by some up-and-coming young executive with an eye on your job.

Pressure rating: High. Responsibility takes its toll and you have to answer to the board. Marketing is a crucial part of any business; if you get it wrong the whole enterprise could crash.

Glamour rating: Depends on the sector and company, but could be very high. If you have good media skills you could find yourself featured in the business press, your comments quoted and your opinions respected.

Travel rating: Could be high. There are international conferences, business meetings, plus visits to overseas factories and distributors. Contrariwise, depending on the firm and your market, could be almost non-existent.

If anyone has to take the blame, the buck stops at this desk. Of course, that means this is also the person who claims all the praise and credit for an effective campaign. Either way, blame or credit, this is the person responsible to the board for the activities of the marketing department. Once, the marketing role was relegated to the bottom of the ranking of directors. These days not only is it regarded as one of the most important, but often the managing director comes from a marketing background.

George Shaw, a marketing veteran who runs a medium-sized marketing consultancy, says, 'Marketing director is usually an in-house title. This is the boss of the marketing department, who at least once a month has to go to board meetings and report on marketing activity. If there is no board seat as part of the job, this person might be referred to as head of marketing.'

The number in the in-house team varies dramatically from one to 30 or 40, depending on the size of the organisation. Sometimes the in-house marketing department will delegate specific marketing tasks, like advertising, PR or promotion, to third party agencies. The reason for this is that they can be fired more easily and they can bring more skills to bear than an in-house team, but the disadvantage is that they often have many other clients and you may find their attention and loyalties torn. But as marketing director you'll be responsible for briefing and managing the freelancers as much as those on the staff.

You'll also have to meet with the product managers and brand managers, to review the status and progress of current campaigns and discuss future projects. You'll work closely with them to ensure that product development meets the marketing objectives and vice versa.

You'll have to commission market research, arrange focus groups and do some discreet sampling and vox popping.

According to George, 'Also much of the time is spent managing staff, recruiting the right people, ensuring that everyone has the right training and career development, managing budgets, planning and scheduling. There is lots of pen-pushing at the senior levels in any department and marketing is no exception. The practical tasks are carried out by the junior staff and if you have recruited the right people that should happen without you having to worry about whether they have been done or whether they have been done right.'

By the time you reach this senior level you will have had several years in marketing. George has been in marketing and PR for over 20 years and knows many marketing professionals. He says, 'Most probably started as a marketing assistant, progressed to executive or manager and eventually became director. You will have picked up lots of hints and tips and understand intuitively by now the processes of creating and running a marketing campaign. You have your own proven techniques for recruiting and managing the right team and keeping them motivated and focused.'

You will understand the products or services of your company extremely well, inside out and upside down. You know all about the history and future plans, the competition and the new products they are developing, as well those in your own research and development (R&D) department. You'll have to carry out a continual **SWOT analysis** in your mind and see every product or service in terms of the **Boston Matrix**. You will be responsible for defining the brand and developing a target market strategy. It will be up to you to set out the objectives of every marketing campaign and ensure that the right team is assigned to run it. You will probably have several campaigns underway at any time, some in advertising, others in promotion, as well as press and direct customer activity. Some projects will be short term, but others may be very long term, running for five years or more – part of the company's strategy for the future.

George adds, 'The marketing director has to understand the importance of retaining existing customers, for it is cheaper to keep a customer than recruit new ones. But they have to be looking for new markets, new customers, the whole time too.'

The marketing director has to take an overall view, according to George. 'They have a grand picture of the products or services, their image and how they should develop.' You are the most likely member of the marketing team to get opportunities to travel. There may be trade shows abroad which you have to visit to see what the market is doing and what your competitors are up to or you might want to exhibit. You might hire a local exhibition agent to set up the stand, but you'll have to be there and available to represent the company.

You'll have to deal with the press and if this strikes fear in your heart then you need to get some media training arranged. There are plenty of one-day courses available, such as the one at www.anniegurton.com. Any journalist wanting to talk to your company about products or services or get your views on industry issues will ask for either the PR manager or the marketing director and, whatever appears in print, you will probably be held responsible for it.

You'll spend lots of time reading trade and industry journals, as well as marketing publications, to develop views on all the issues and trends of the time. If the marketing director can get quoted in the media, the business benefits (it's not bad for the marketing director's career either). So media awareness and an appreciation of how to use the media for free publicity are skills that the rest of the board will expect.

Skills you'll need

- People management comes high on the list, but the skills of diplomacy and the ability to motivate can be acquired over several years as a marketing assistant, executive and manager.
- Financial acumen is vital, not only to manage marketing projects within budget but also to understand the costings of the products and services you are marketing. You don't just have to be able to read a spreadsheet, you have to understand all financial workings, financial statements, statistics and charts.

- You'll need computer expertise at the desktop level as well as an appreciation of how networks help marketing applications and an understanding of the Internet, not just as an office tool but as a marketing tool too. The Internet is now an important marketing channel and Internet marketing is different from traditional techniques.
- You'll have to negotiate a lot, so although you won't actually be selling you'll have to understand the principles of sales and know how to get what you want. You'll have to negotiate budgets and timescales, sometimes with other internal people and sometimes with third parties. The more you can get what you want, while at the same time leaving the other party thinking they got the best deal, the better.
- You need to begin developing your relationship with the press as soon as you start in marketing. You'll need to know how to fend off awkward questions and how to promote the company and its products without being too obvious about it, so get some training if you are unsure what their agenda is or how to deal with them.
- A good marketing director has to have outstanding communication and management skills, be reliable, conscientious and efficient, never miss a deadline, and strive for the highest possible standard. The sooner you start to work with those aims in mind, the better.

Tips

- George says, 'If you are ambitious and you've got your eye on a marketing directorship you need to start developing the skills as soon as you can. Get as much training as you can and watch and learn from those you work for. Try to get some professional marketing qualifications – there are plenty that can be done part-time, including the Open University. While you are working your way up, take any courses you can on presentation and communication skills, both personal and technical. You need to know how to work an audience and how to manage the technology to support a presentation.'
- Reputations – good and bad – start early, so have high professional and personal ethics and be scrupulous in all your activities, business and personal, if you are aiming for a directorship.
- Even if you think you can do a better job than the director you work for, don't let it show.
- The director is the leader and should innovate rather than just administer, should be an original rather than just a copy,

should develop campaigns instead of maintaining them. You'll need a long-range perspective rather than a short-range view, so keep your eye on the horizon.

■ The director rarely accepts the status quo, but always strives to do the right thing.

Glossary

■ **Boston Matrix**
A theory developed by the Boston Consulting Group which categorises products according to their stage in their life cycle. Products are called either falling stars, cash cows, problem children or rising stars, with a strategy for marketing, pricing and promotion for each.

■ **SWOT analysis**
An analysis of a company's or product's strengths, weaknesses, opportunities and threats as a means of developing a well-rounded strategy.

Marketing manager

Money: Depending on your previous experience, from about £15,000 to about £35,000. Perks depend on the products you are marketing, but you'll probably get some samples. Most likely you'll be able to go along on customer hospitality event outings, which may be trips to the opera, rounds of golf or paintballing. Remember to let the customer win.

Hours: Fairly regular, probably 9–5, unless there is a rush on or a campaign is reaching its peak. If the director wants to get home and there is work to be done, volunteer.

Health risk: Low.

Pressure rating: Low but rising. As you become more experienced and take on more responsibility you'll find the pressure will grow. There is always pressure to do a good job.

Glamour rating: Depends on the company and the market sector. Working for a washing machine company has less pulling power than working for a mobile phone company or a pop band. If you want glamour, pick your industry carefully.

Travel rating: Low to medium. The director or senior marketing managers will take their pick of the best trips. You can hope to be asked to man a stall at a trade conference abroad, but it will be more hard work than pleasure.

*Some call themselves marketing managers, some marketing executives. Sometimes companies have both and usually in that case the manager is senior to the executive. Whatever you are called, this could be your first or second job in in-house marketing. If you want a glamorous career in marketing, this is where you pick your employer carefully – a marketing job in the finance or **FMCG** sector will probably be less interesting than marketing in the entertainment or film industry. Your choice now will affect the rest of your career. Whichever firm you work for, your tasks will be wide ranging and you'll get it in the neck if you make mistakes, but it's fun and rewarding and you'll learn lots.*

The marketing executive or manager (we'll use manager here) is one of a team and the chances are you'll move around, learning the different aspects of marketing as you go. You might spend some time on advertising, direct mail, customer support or PR and promotion. All the jobs have the same basic requirements – good communications skills and careful attention to detail.

David West has been a marketing consultant for many years

after a career in the marketing department of a leading IT company. He says, 'If there is a marketing assistant you'll be spared the most lowly jobs, but if not you could find yourself stuffing envelopes or faxing distributors with price changes or opening competition entries from customers. The marketing department embraces a huge range of jobs and as marketing manager you'll be expected to be able to do them all. Even if outside third parties are used for specific specialist jobs like advertising, market research or press relations, you'll have to help manage them and work with them and you can't do that unless you know what they are supposed to be doing.'

Depending on the size of the company there may be several other marketing managers or executives or you may be running the marketing department single-handed. Either way, you'll have to be a jack of all trades, able to read and run a spreadsheet, commission market research and understand the results and appreciate how your company's products or services are placed in the big wide world against its competitors. You'll know its strengths and weaknesses and you'll understand the need for discretion when future product strategies and marketing campaigns are developed.

According to David, the marketing and sales functions used to be very closely linked – in some firms even now, the marketing manager is the sales manager – but the jobs are very different. 'You will have to plan a sales strategy and work with the sales team to carry it through. There are close links between the two teams, even if they are separated.

'You'll learn all about **market segmentation** and customer profiling and how to market to existing customers according to the information you learn about them from their past buying patterns.'

With the rest of the marketing team, you'll be developing a strategy and seeing it through. You'll have to understand the brand profile and know how to develop it to meet the expectations of the customer profile, which will probably be different for every product or service that your company provides.

David says that as marketing manager you'll take buzzwords like 'reliability', 'efficiency', 'caring customer support', 'innovation', 'friendly', 'established' and 'professional' and create a marketing campaign which helps reinforce these in the minds of the consumers. 'The campaign will reinforce and reiterate all these buzzwords, so that when a consumer hears the company name or the brand, those are the images they associate with it,' he adds.

You'll have to develop an appropriate marketing mix for the product, which will be a balance between the **4 Ps** and the different media and marketing techniques. So you'll have to make sure that the marketing at point of sale is right for the target audience and so forth.

The Internet is an increasingly important part of marketing these days. It offers a way for you to deliver marketing messages direct to the computers of your existing and potential customers and Internet marketing has some special requirements you'll have to learn. It's not just about knowing how to use a computer – that will be expected anyway – it's about how the Internet can be used for marketing in a positive, successful way. You have to know that you can't **spam** people and expect them to buy, but there are some excellent techniques for developing better customer relationships.

David says that the marketing manager's primary objectives are to raise the profile of the firm's products or services, help set sales forecasts and help define the best way to reach potential customers. 'To do this you need an analytical and intelligent mind, able to read reports and surveys and come to conclusions which effect the best type of marketing campaign.'

Once decisions have been made, budgets set and tasks assigned, the hard work begins. It will be pressurised and very varied and the amount of responsibility you are given will directly reflect your competence and reliability at doing the job.

Skills you'll need

- You'll need a combination of hard skills, supported by certificates and accreditations, and soft skills, meaning you know how to work with people and communicate effectively. Soft skills also include presentation techniques, motivation and teamwork with those around you.
- You'll have to have an eye for detail and be conscientious about doing a good job. If you can demonstrate that you are reliable and never let people down and are enthusiastic without being irritating, you'll fit in with other marketing types.
- Basic computer word-processing and e-mail skills will be all you need, but expect to learn more computer skills as you go along. You may not know how to use a spreadsheet or presentation software when you start, but you'll be expected to learn.
- You'll have to take care of practical details and make sure that the freelancers and third parties are doing what they are supposed to do, in good time.
- You'll have to look smart and know what is appropriate behaviour for different situations. Some firms will want you to wear a suit all the time, but usually marketing departments are viewed as creative and smart casual dress is acceptable, except for special heavyweight meetings. The more junior you are, the more careful you have to be to get the dress code right – casual doesn't mean party-wear and most professional offices expect long-sleeved clothes most of the time.

- David says, 'Remember that marketing departments are often a mass of egos and creative energies and sometimes it is best to take a slow, self-deprecating, modest approach until you know everybody and understand the dynamics. Keep the jokes about the managing director until you've been there six months.'
- 'Volunteer to have a go at all the marketing skills and don't be afraid to roll your sleeves up and take on any task. It's all experience,' recommends David.
- Put yourself forward to get as many professional qualifications as you can, but don't come back from a marketing course and start telling everyone else what they should be doing. You need to balance classroom marketing theory with practical experience. Every market and company is different and often experience counts far more than classroom theory.
- Don't be surprised if the director takes your suggestions and passes them off as their own or takes credit for your work. It's not good practice, but take it as a lesson on what not to do when you reach director level. It goes on and you have to accept it.
- The manager has to maintain the defined campaign and is not expected to be creative or innovative. Make sure you do things right and keep your eye on the detail.

Glossary

- **FMCG**
  Fast-moving consumer goods, which includes products like washing powder and foods.
- **4 Ps**
  A specific combination of marketing elements is used to achieve an organisation or the objectives of individuals and satisfy the target market, usually having four major variables: product, promotion, price and place (location).
- **Market segmentation**
  The process of subdividing a market into distinct subsets of customers who behave in similar ways and have similar values, incomes or needs.
- **Spam (mail)**
  Unsolicited marketing information sent by e-mail. The origins of the term are unclear, but are probably something to do with the ubiquitous pink luncheon meat which at one time appeared in salads everywhere. A spam list is created from marketing and direct sales lists. Individuals can arrange to have their names removed from spam lists.

Media analyst

Money: Depends enormously on experience, but people rarely move into analysis straight from university. It usually takes an apprenticeship in planning or buying, so it won't be a first job. You'll probably start on £18,000, and this could rise to £40,000 working for a specialist consultancy. You'll be judged on the clarity of your analysis and recommendations.

Hours: Routine. Probably 9–5 or 10–6. There is unlikely to be much need for overtime.

Health risk: Minimal. You'll be instructing others to put posters on billboards and hoardings – the most you'll have to do is load the video.

Pressure rating: Subtle, but medium. On a day-to-day level the pressure rating might seem low, but overall it is medium or even high, because entire campaigns and a great deal of money could depend on your getting the analysis, recommendations and post-campaign feedback right.

Glamour rating: Low. Actually this is one of the more interesting jobs in marketing for the cerebral type, but when you tell your granny what you do she'll probably say, 'What?'

Travel rating: Low. You may have to go to exhibitions to plan the siting of ads and make recommendations on the best site and see the effect of your and other companies' advertising, but otherwise you'll be reading newspapers and magazines, watching TV, listening to the radio and surfing the Internet – all jobs that can be done in the office. You'll have to attend client meetings and liaise with other marketing professionals, but this will rarely require significant journeys.

The range of options for advertising strategies is enormous and growing. How does the marketer decide where the advertisements will be placed and for how long? Which medium appeals best to which target audience? These are things that are a mystery to you and me, but the media analyst knows and can tell you with their eyes shut.

James Kirk has been working as a media analyst for a large marketing agency for ten years, starting straight after his A levels. He says, 'I love it. There is lots of variety and I particularly like the research side, when we have to check all the new sorts of media.' These include all kinds of non-personal communications channels, including print media (newspapers, magazines and direct mail), broadcast media (radio, television and now the Internet) and display media (billboards, signs and posters).

Part of James's job is to monitor all the new sites, magazines, publications and Internet opportunities. He says, 'Sometimes I have to read a new magazine, look at the media pack sent out by the media sales team which explains the target audience of the magazine and then make a report on how valuable I think it will be for certain clients and advise whether they should be advertising there.'

James often has meetings with clients, as well as other marketing professionals in the consultancy, although he says that the job is largely a back-office one. 'In the beginning I didn't meet many people and just made lots of cups of tea and coffee. But gradually I became more confident and experienced, and now I'm able to make recommendations to marketing consultants and their clients about the best media mix.'

Rarely does a marketing campaign use only one medium. James usually starts with a budget and a target audience and then puts together a proposal. He says, 'The first thing is to determine the objectives, which may be to raise the profile of a brand or inform people about a price change. Or it may be to change brand beliefs or create brand sympathy or just to persuade them to get to the shops as soon as possible and buy!' To evaluate different media for different objectives, James has to use existing data and perhaps also commission new market research. He says, 'I use a scale for the various levels of impact of the different media to different audiences. For example, consumers might be satisfied or bored, accepting or apathetic, sympathetic or rejecting; they might notice a message or they might easily forget. We ask whether they will buy, repeat buy, have any intention of buying, whether their attitudes have changed or whether they are still unaware of a product after exposure to advertising.'

Timing of advertisements in the different media is another thing that James studies. He says, 'The marketing and advertising schedule changes over the course of a year. Some products peak in December and drop in March, others peak during the school holidays, others are the opposite. It depends on the product and the customer. It is very fascinating.' Depending on his view, advertisements are scheduled either to run continuously over a given period or are pulsed, placed in bursts to catch the decision-making periods.

James also has to compare the different types of media vehicle, bearing in mind the target audience and budget. He says, 'Each has limitations as well as advantages. For example, billboards have no audience selectivity and the creativity can be limited, but it is a low-cost option with high repeat exposure.

On the other hand, television offers high reach and high attention, although it is fleeting exposure and high cost.'

Much of James's work remains to be done after each campaign. He will liaise with the planner and buyer before the campaign, but afterwards will spend considerable time examining and re-examining the effect and potency of each media vehicle, deciding on the value.

The media analyst has to create detailed reports for the marketing professionals and their clients and the media planners and buyers, which evaluate the characteristics and costs of the media options. The report will also include details of audience size, potential exposure and its quality, audience traits for each medium, legal restrictions, the best type of message for each medium and how these fit in with the objectives, brand image and message of each product. James also has to recommend the best strategy to achieve the goal of reaching the largest desirable audience at the most efficient cost. He has to create a written document, which is distributed by Internet to the closed group of interested parties, but also has to make presentations on his findings and judgments. He says, 'I used to hate having to stand up in front of a group of clients talking through the recommendations I'd be making to the planners and buyers, but I'm used to it now. I would recommend anyone thinking of going into marketing to do a public-speaking course or join the debating society at university. I didn't and it took me a long time to catch up on the skills.'

He adds, 'I love my work because it has a balance of intellectual rigour, logic and an element of gambling. It is not a precise science and all I can ever do it make the best recommendation based on experience and common sense.'

Sometimes the job of media analyst is combined with media planning and/or buying, but in the consultancy that James works for there are enough clients and enough advertising and marketing campaigns to keep him busy with the analysis alone. He says, 'I am currently applying for a new job which will include planning and media buying. It is for a smaller agency and all three jobs are rolled into one, and I will be working with other people who are doing all three tasks. But some people prefer to keep the tasks separate.'

Skills you'll need

- James say that confidence in public speaking and presentation is vital and he's also pleased that he learned to analyse data and statistics.
- Employers will be looking for the ability to 'plan your work and work to plan', so through your school coursework and

career after college or university, you should demonstrate the ability to be a self-starter. Even though supervision and training are available, a media analyst will probably come from a career as a planner or buyer, so by the time you become an analyst you'll already know quite a lot about the different sorts of media.

■ You'll have to be proactive, with the gumption to look for new media vehicles and analyse their potential for particular clients.

Tips

■ You'll probably be moving across to media analyst from a spell as a planner or buyer, so identify the companies you'd like to work for and the people you need on your side.

■ If you know a media analyst, spend time with them to understand better the subtleties of the job.

■ If you are still at university and thinking about a career as a media analyst, you should be a media junkie – read as many different types and categories of newspaper and magazine as you can, trying to identify the differences between them and the market each is aimed at.

Media buyer

Money: Unlike media sellers, who are on basic and commission, buyers usually command a realistic living wage. It could start at £15,000 and rise to £35,000, depending on the budget and the prestige of the client you are buying space for.

Hours: Regular. There may be frequent after-hours entertainment, usually on the expense account of the media sales teams, and they will all be keen to entertain you in the evenings. You'll feel like the flavour of the week.

Health risk: Apart from the risk of over-indulgence from the expense account hospitality that media sales managers are keen to lavish on you, there is very little risk. This is an office-, telephone- and PC-based job and apart from the aforementioned hospitality, there is little danger to your health.

Pressure rating: High. Negotiations will be intense, with deadlines and time constraints as well as budgetary restrictions. The media sales teams will be trying to get as much money out of you for the worst sites and spaces, while you'll be trying to get the best you can.

Glamour rating: Low to medium. The media sales teams will treat you as though you are royalty, but few people outside the industry will know what a media buyer does.

Travel rating: Low. The furthest you will go will be to the local hostelry or club for sustenance, courtesy of the media salesperson currently trying to persuade you to book with them.

The people who place advertisements are called media buyers and sellers, depending on which side of the fence they sit. Those working for media such as magazines and television companies are salespeople and their job is called media sales. Those working for the marketing firms are called media buyers. Both sides are often represented by specialist agencies which have the best negotiating skills.

When the media analysts have decided on a strategy it's left to the media buyers to get the most effective advertising for the budget. Jane Simmons has been a media buyer for a large marketing company for five years. She says, 'The media sales team have to get as much revenue or "yield" as they can for each page, half-page or quarter-page or minute on the airwaves. So there is a game going on, with lots of negotiating to arrive at a final price which everyone feels happy with. The best outcome is if everyone feels like they have done well and driven a hard bargain – it's called a win-win situation. Sometimes one side will feel that they gave in too soon or compromised or paid too much, and although they will stick to the deal they won't feel happy about it. That is satisfactory business, because they'll pay for what they've agreed, but it's not the best result. If everyone feels happy, not only is that deal the best possible but there will be a good basis for further deals in the future.'

Some publications cost less than others to advertise in, although the cheaper the medium, the less high-profile or smaller their audience. And within each media format there are some areas which cost more than others. The back cover or inside front cover of a magazine, for example, or the slot halfway through the TV or radio news, is going to cost more than something 'near the back' of a magazine or broadcast in the middle of the night. There are always premium publications and programmes and premium slots within each one.

So media buying and media selling are two sides of the same coin. Jane says, 'Obviously, different products need different strategies. A child's toy, for example, will require magazines targeted at the kids' market plus TV slots in children's prime time. Weekends are good times for children's advertising – the middle of the night is not, unless you are aiming at those who are actually going to buy the products. The target customer will be agreed with the brand manager by the media analyst when they are working out the strategy.'

Jane likes the bargaining and negotiating aspect of the job. 'It's quite exhilarating,' she says. 'There are always lots of "special" deals and agreements going on.

Relationships between buyers and sellers are very important and often deals will link together several product strategies. They might also spread over several issues or publications and one media buyer might get a better price for one purchase by linking it to an agreement to fill another less popular slot. There is always a lot of horse-trading going on, much of it in restaurants and bars. Some say that back-handers are sometimes offered by sellers to buyers to persuade them to buy space in certain new or difficult media, but that's probably just malicious gossip. Jane refused to comment on kick-backs and back-handers.

As you become more proficient at purchasing and can drive a better bargain, getting the best spaces for the lowest cost, you will get promoted. Having started as an assistant or executive, you'll progress to manager and eventually head up several teams.

Most media buyers work on salary while media sellers are on commission or a mix of salary and commission.

Media buying has traditionally been done on the telephone, but these days the Internet is increasingly important.

Those selling space post the spaces available and the rates on a website and buyers book those they want. However, most nitty-gritty wheeling and dealing still goes on either on the telephone or in person and relies a lot on personal relationships. Not many delicate deals are closed on the web, but it is a good place to start negotiations. Jane says, 'I couldn't use the Internet at all when I started this job and I didn't have a PC on my desk, but now I have and I use the Internet all the time. It is a valuable tool, but it doesn't replace the personal relationship that I develop with the people who sell media space.'

Skills you'll need

- First and foremost, you must be able to negotiate. Media buying is partly about strategic thinking but mostly about driving a hard bargain. Deals can be complex, covering several different media vehicles and even several clients too, so you'll need to be able to think on your feet and keep things in your head.
- Relationships will be important, so good people skills are vital.
- You'll have to be able to match the demands of the client or product manager with the media vehicles available for the budget allocated. Sometimes the product manager expects a higher profile campaign than you are able to arrange and you'll have to persuade him or her that you've got the best possible exposure for the money available.
- You might have to handle conflicts. If you buy space on behalf of clients and the magazine, TV programme or bill poster company gets it wrong, you'll have to arrange a rebate and argue compensation, as well as pacify the client. And they often do get things wrong, so this might be a skill you frequently have to use.
- With pan-European marketing campaigns you'll have to negotiate media purchases in other countries. The lingua franca is English, but it always helps if you can discuss and negotiate in the local language. So French and German, at least, will be a great advantage.
- If you are media buying from foreign sellers, you'll have to be able to make fast currency conversions in your head – getting it wrong could be very costly and embarrassing.

Tips

- Polish your Internet surfing skills and make sure that you are proficient in appropriate languages, spoken if not written.
- Practise negotiating – ironically, the best way to learn good negotiation skills is by selling media space, so a holiday job in the media sales department of the local newspaper, for

example, would put you streets ahead in an interview and give you a comprehensive view of what media buying is all about.

- Jane says, 'When you are just a consumer you don't consciously notice the media vehicles or think about the different advertisements that each carries. When I was thinking about a career in media buying, back at university, I started by making notes about the different media and the types of advertisements they each carried. I got a few media packs from the magazines to see how each tried to sell itself and then compared their claims with the reality of the magazines. It's an interesting and useful exercise.'

Media planner

Money: Varies, but usually from £18,000 to £40,000, depending on experience and seniority. You may be able to negotiate the usual corporate perks when you are very experienced and the agency or client doesn't want to lose you but isn't willing to give you more money. Some media sales managers believe it is as important to smooth the path to the planners as it is to the buyers and will wine you and dine you on their expense account. Enjoy, but don't let it affect your judgment.

Hours: Routine, with little need for overtime except occasional corporate hospitality. Usually 9–5 or 10–6.

Health risk: About as low as it can be.

Pressure rating: Medium. You have a serious responsibility to get it right or the entire marketing budget is wasted. No matter how good the advertisements, if they appear in the wrong place at the wrong time, the money may as well have been flushed down the lavatory.

Glamour rating: Low outside the marketing and media world. Most people won't know what you do. But medium inside the industry – those who know what planners do and understand the importance of the job will show great respect.

Travel rating: Low, except to the local pub after work.

It's only in really big consultancies or agencies that this is a separate function from that of media analyst and media buyer. Usually the planning role is undertaken by the analyst or buyer as part of their job.

Being responsible for planning how an advertising campaign will run is challenging, requiring a skilful and complex appreciation of many different factors. Paul Skinner, who works for one of the large American-owned multinational marketing agencies, says, 'I used to like playing "Go" at school and I'm sure that's why I like media planning. The long-range thinking and having to juggle lots of things in your mind are very similar.'

Paul's job doesn't just require him to make decisions about which media vehicles are best for particular products or services: he also has to decide the timings of each. So, for example, in a campaign lasting six months for the launch of a new product aimed at the female teenage market, he will suggest a high-profile brand awareness-raising campaign in teen magazines at the beginning, with most concentration on TV at the peak teen viewing times as the campaign progresses. 'You want to catch

How to get into Marketing and PR

the wave of interest that's created when some of the teenagers start to use the product. There is hopefully some self-seeding of the market when the early adopters start using it and talking about it and you need to reinforce the fashion-conscious "must-have" factor that that can create.'

But he points out that a product or service aimed at the **grey market** will need different timings and media. 'Many grey consumers watch TV in the daytime, so during school term times we'll spend more on grey market TV advertising.' Paul adds that the grey market is increasingly IT and Internet literate and can be reached through Internet advertising as effectively as young people can. 'The grey market can afford to get the latest computers in their homes, while young people might just have mobile phones, so for them we'll concentrate on **WAP** messaging and use the Internet for holiday, insurance and car advertising for older people.'

Media planning is almost exclusively a back-office job and Paul says that he rarely has a chance to get away from his desk. 'I have to read and write a lot of reports and like a nice quiet space to work from.' His employer is happy for him to work from home, which he likes. 'There is plenty of flexibility in my working hours and location,' he says. 'I can also wear what I like to work, which suits me.'

Not all employers are as flexible or easy-going as Paul's and many require you to be at the office every day. Provided you have a computer and telephone, it doesn't really matter where you are, though. Paul says, 'When I started I had to learn the theory of media planning, which is more of a science in the USA. As the firm I work for is American, they wanted me to work the way they do. But I'm very glad I did. It has given me a very good set of methodologies to work from and I've found that over here the techniques are far more hit and miss.'

The media planner's goal is to achieve the best possible audience at the most effective cost. Paul has to balance the objectives of the product and brand managers with the budgets they have allocated for the marketing and the part of the budget that the marketing manager has allocated to advertising. He is also responsible for planning the different promotional campaigns and the timing of the direct marketing campaigns to tie them in with the advertising. He says, 'When I started we used manual project management systems, but now we use software to plan campaigns. Everything we do also has to be tied up with the activities of other marketing professionals, like the art director, the print buyer, the production people and those on the ground who go out and put billboards up. A single simple media decision can involve several different teams and many people.'

Paul likes the fact that his working environment is fairly quiet. 'I'm just left to get on with it and I like working on my own,' he says. In other marketing organisations where media planning is part of the media buying and analysis role, there is no quiet back-room job. Paul says, 'When I was working in media sales I knew I wanted to move into planning and worked on my own to develop the skills and understanding of what a media planner does.' He believes that studying part-time and being a self-starting student helped when he applied for the job he has now. 'They liked the fact that I'd shown initiative and started finding out about media planning on my own. I think it indicated that I was the right sort of personality for the job.'

Since he got his job Paul has not been on any formal training courses and he doesn't think there is anything that a course could teach him. 'I don't want to sound arrogant, but the in-house training was excellent and now I learn and upgrade my knowledge from day to day, on the job. The only thing I might do is a course in statistics and economics, which would help in the analysis part of my job.'

One challenge facing Paul is how to measure the return on investment in certain media vehicles against others. 'The trouble is that one can never have a blind or control situation, in which the plan I devise is compared with others. It can't be done. So it is almost impossible to say definitely that one aspect of a plan is better than another or that different timing would have worked better. You learn to be intuitive about the effectiveness of the value of some media and certain timescales against others, but there is no paradigm for measurement. I think every media planner uses some published methodologies combined with their own experience.'

Indirect benefits from advertising are also important and Paul has to take them into account. 'I think the justification for advertising is evolving and if the reason why people advertise is changing, then the way that we advertise should also adapt with time.' For example, he says, a media plan designed to enhance **brand equity** in the long term should be different from a plan designed to generate incremental sales in the short or medium term.

Some media planners use the same plan across the whole of the country or even across Europe, especially if the media planner has to double up as media buyer. But when it becomes a specialist discipline it becomes more scientific and detailed, according to Paul.

With the balance of returns from different media continuing to change, the plans being proposed also change. Television, for example, is a cheaper and different medium to what it was a few years ago. Among the variables are regional differences, and vertical market differences in the product or service audience. The relative value of TV varies dramatically across the UK, by more than a factor of two between London and the northern regions and Paul has to understand all the permutations when working out the best plan. 'I love thinking about the different personalities and profiles of customers in different areas, different cultures, different factors that affect them in different ways.

'When I'm talking about a media plan to the product or brand manager, the first thing they will be wanting is a return on the investment of their marketing budget and that's what I have to try and promise them.'

Skills you'll need

- This job suits those who prefer to be away from the marketing and PR limelight, working in the back office.
- You'll need high-level analytical and planning skills – Paul's hobby of playing 'Go' stood him in good stead.
- You'll need to be able to read complex reports and surveys and translate a client's vague list of requirements into a practical strategic plan.

Tips

- You may not be a front-office worker, liaising all the time with clients or the public, but don't forget basic sartorial rules. Dressing down isn't a licence to lose all sense of professionalism.
- Take up strategic planning games, such as 'Go' or chess. They'll develop your ability to think ahead, plan, and carry lots of ideas in your head at the same time.

Glossary

- **Brand equity**
  The value of a brand. Something like Coca-Cola has very high brand equity whereas Bloggs Brothers' squash doesn't. As a brand becomes more well known and respected, its equity rises, although there is no formal, tangible way of measuring this equity.
- **Grey market**
  Retired people or people over 50 years old. (Not to be confused with the grey market of illicit unauthorised products.)
- **WAP technology**
  Wireless application protocol, likely to be the biggest leap in communications since the advent of the mobile phone. It allows individuals to log onto the Internet from any location, using their mobile or desktop PC, accessing data that may be personally tailored.

New media director / producer / manager / executive

Money: Varies depending on seniority and experience, but generally any new media jobs pay more than their traditional equivalents.

Hours: Again, they vary according to seniority and level of responsibility, but usually new media workers are expected to be highly flexible in their timekeeping. They often have portables or PCs at home and are expected to work out of conventional office hours.

Health risk: Low.

Pressure rating: Again, varies according to seniority and personality, but the more you get paid the more pressure you can expect.

Glamour rating: Medium. Any job connected with the Internet commands more respect that the traditional equivalents.

Travel rating: Low. You might have to travel to a client's office or go to an exhibition or seminar to catch up on what others are doing, but the whole point about new media is that you don't have to travel to stay in touch. Teleconferencing and webcams are replacing face-to-face meetings.

*'New media' generally means the Internet, but also includes other radical ways to get marketing messages across, such as **WAP** devices, **push technology** and 'viral' or 'virus' marketing (see **Viral marketer**). At the cutting edge of marketing, professionals in this field often have to take old principles and strategic approaches and turn them on their head.*

In the electronic world all is not what it seems and nothing is accepted as conventional. As soon as a technique becomes widespread, it is ready to be changed. Everything adapts quickly and the job of the new media team is to keep up or stay one step ahead. Sebastian Grey is a new media specialist, writing banner ads and devising campaigns that give rewards to consumers who respond.

He says, 'The trick is looking at old products and services and turning them into new messages delivered by new means. You still need to be creative and able to see a strategy through from concept to post-campaign assessment and review, but you also need to be able to challenge the rule book and keep the brands fresh.'

You have to understand the technologies you are working with, says Sebastian, and that means keeping up with innovations. 'I frequently work with WAP,' he says, 'and that means thinking up campaigns which can be translated into quick messages for display on mobile phones.' Recently Sebastian was working with a chain of pubs on messages which would be relayed to all consumers within a certain age group, telling them of a special price offer on an imported lager. 'It would be sent to all phone users within that age profile, who were within a mile of one of the pubs.'

The problem is that the life cycle of new media campaigns is extremely rapid. Sebastian says, 'Mention banner advertising to most clients these days and they are likely to be extremely cynical. Research shows that it has a low score for effectiveness, but it is still necessary to include it as part of a campaign as a way of raising awareness of a brand.'

Banner advertising, however, is a poor indicator of the health of the new media as a means of promoting products and services, building brands and reaching customers. Sebastian says, 'New media has to be part of a cohesive marketing strategy and the basics still apply when it comes to profiling your target market, understanding the consumer's buying process and establishing your market objectives.' The great pitfall of new media marketing, he adds, is failure to co-ordinate on-line with off-line marketing. 'Co-ordination ensures a consistent brand strategy, creating stronger consumer awareness and complementary marketing propositions.'

Brainstorming to come up with new ideas is a small but ongoing part of the job, says Sebastian. 'Ideas can come at any time, but we also have sessions when we sit around and try to thrash out some original concepts. After that, the hard work comes in the planning and ensuring that we choose the right new media vehicles and techniques to achieve the clients' objectives. The ideal is a broad mix of on-line techniques, of which banner advertising is an element.'

The new media professionals have to work with the technical programmers, for example to ensure that search engines are optimised for the campaign and client, and with the PR professionals, strategic sales channels and sales partnerships managers and affiliate and third-party partnership managers. 'There is always a complex route for the product to take to get to market and the new media campaign manager has to understand all these and the politics of each and make the marketing campaign appropriate for each and fit in with other marketing initiatives.'

Sebastian says that e-mail is a crucial element of new media, but has to be used carefully. 'People are wary of **spamming**, and of course there are laws restricting any mass e-mailing. But e-mails can be a very good way of getting people to respond to a banner ad or any other form of marketing.' He specialises in developing personalised campaigns, using e-**CRM** technology (electronic customer relationship management), which allows him to identify every target customer.

Sebastian explains that he came to new media marketing by an unconventional route. 'I'd done my A levels and I got a job to help me pay my way through university with a marketing consultancy. I loved it and they liked me and persuaded me to put off going to university, where I had a place to do business studies.' After a year, the same thing happened, with Sebastian being offered a middle management marketing job with a salary of £20,000 a year. He says, 'I was concerned about not getting a degree qualification but the salary, plus the thought that when my contemporaries left university I would already have been in the world of work for three years, made me give up the idea of leaving the job to study.' He says that he has learned more on the job than he could have at university. 'New media is such a new science that there are no courses specialising in it.' He is studying part-time and already has one serious marketing qualification and is working on a second. 'I find that having a job says more than any qualification, although they are extremely useful and, of course, you learn a lot of theory on the courses, which is invaluable.'

Sebastian is concerned that if he ever wants to move to another agency, the lack of a degree might count against him, but adds, 'I think the fact that I have been doing the job, working in new media, I have analytical and presentation skills learned on the job, I can demonstrate the ability to work with colleagues and clients, count more than any qualification. I think I had a lucky break to be offered a job and I would have been mad to pass up the opportunity.' However, Sebastian is right to be concerned – if an employer is faced with two or three suitable candidates for a job they *will* look at their academic qualifications and grades, because they are still seen to be the best way of evaluating raw intelligence, however much experience counts.

New media marketing is a new science – as it matures we can expect to see increasing creativity in the planning and execution of ideas. Sebastian says, 'At the moment we are still trying to establish the best way of measuring responses and audiences and getting evidence of return on investment. In theory, on-line marketing can be tracked more closely and effectively than any other form of marketing, but there is still doubt in the minds of some clients and senior marketing directors that it has validity.'

Skills you'll need

- Good understanding of new technologies, including **HTML** programming, even though you may not have to do any programming yourself – you'll have to know what the limitations and possibilities are.
- Your main job will be understanding the consumers as well as how to reach them, so your principal focus should be on classic marketing theory skills as well as new media marketing skills. The customers and target markets are the same – even the most IT-literate people have the same desires and needs as their less IT-literate brethren, which the new media team will try to tap into.
- Sebastian says that having a degree of humility helps. 'There is no one with more than a few years' experience at new media marketing and many new media marketers fall into the trap of arrogance. They believe they are the glory pack of marketing that others respect and envy. So the ability to manage your ego will set you apart from many in the field.'

Tips

- Use the Internet and have a WAP phone and see how they are being used for marketing. Get into the habit of forming an opinion on whether a campaign or promotion is successful and then question what the thinking process was that led to the campaign. Try to establish what the assumptions were about the audience. Put yourself in the marketers' shoes and try to imagine how they picture the consumer.
- You are a consumer. When a campaign works for you, try to think what it is about it that appeals to you. Equally, when you see an advertising or promotional campaign that irritates, try to pinpoint exactly what it is about it that rubs you up the wrong way.
- Try to work in an environment that encourages creativity by making sure that people have the confidence and freedom to express themselves. Avoid environments that are hierarchical and which reward years in the job rather than brilliant ideas and the ability to execute them.

- **Customer relationship management (CRM)**
  The management of existing customers to ensure their loyalty.
- **HTML**
  Hypertext mark-up language, a computer programming language used specifically for developing websites.
- **Push technology**
  The ability to send unsolicited information and marketing, probably based on previous buying patterns and declared interests, to prospective customers electronically. Particularly used for e-mail and WAP marketing.
- **Spam mail**
  Unsolicited marketing information sent by e-mail. The origins of the term are unclear, but are probably something to do with the ubiquitous pink luncheon meat which at one time appeared in salads everywhere. A spam list is created from marketing and direct sales lists. Individuals can arrange to have their names removed from spam lists.
- **WAP technology**
  Wireless application protocol, likely to be the biggest leap in communications since the advent of the mobile phone. It allows individuals to log onto the Internet from any location, using their mobile or desktop PC, accessing data that may be personally tailored.

On-line marketing manager

See *E-commerce marketing manager, Internet marketing manager* and *New media director / producer / manager / executive.*

Packaging designer

Money: Probably starting on £12,000 as a junior, rising to £18,000 after three years out of college. More if you work for a large agency, but you're unlikely to earn more than £30,000. Perks are limited and depend on the products you're designing packages for.

Hours: Regular.

Health risk: Low. What damage can a sweet package cause?

Pressure rating: Medium. The whole marketing campaign can stand or fall on the product packaging, so the pressure is always on to interpret the requirements accurately, design an eye-catching and appropriate package and keep updating it to maintain the brand's position.

Glamour rating: Low. However you say it, packaging designer is never going to be a glamorous job title.

Travel rating: Low. Sometimes you'll have to go to a client meeting or to the marketing agency or to meet the market researchers. Possibly you'll even go out when they are testing the product designs on an audience. But most of the time you'll be at your desk, drawing or using the computer to create new designs.

A graphics design background is usually the path into the specialist area of packaging design, where you'll be working with all kinds of materials and products. It can be a crucial factor in a product's success – in fact, to many marketing professionals, packaging is the fifth 'p' after price, product, place and promotion.

Kate White took the graphics design route, spending three years at college after GCSEs, and then went straight to a specialist design agency that does nothing but develop wrappers and packages for all kinds of goods. 'I started as a junior and spent time working in all the different departments,' she says. 'It was a kind of apprenticeship and the money was very low at the beginning.' Now, after three years, Kate is sufficiently experienced to take on her own projects.

'We work for a variety of clients and each has a wide set of needs and objectives,' she continues. Her last year of college involved a marketing specialisation, learning how to translate marketing and brand objectives into the packaging graphics. 'Each target audience has different preferences and I have to appeal to each and still retain the unique brand characteristics,' she says.

Packaging has many functions which Kate has to consider. As well as protecting goods from damage, it helps keep them fresh and is necessary for labelling and information reasons. 'If a product is to be sold in a self-service outlet, it must by law contain certain information, as well as performing specific sales tasks like attracting attention and selling itself. Rising consumer affluence means that consumers are willing to pay more for the convenience, appearance, dependability and prestige of better packets,' she adds.

Good packaging can create instant consumer recognition of the product, company or brand. In a highly competitive environment like a supermarket, the package may be the client's last chance to influence the customer. 'So we use the package to communicate brand values through the graphics,' says Kate. It also has to appeal to the market segment at which it is targeted and be right for the channel through which it will reach its market.

Kate was involved in the design of an innovative package for a brand of confectionery, which makes it stand out on the shelves. 'The products with unique, distinctive and easily identifiable packages enjoy good recall in market research and are the favourites of the customers,' she says. The reverse is also true, with poorly designed packaging consigning a perfectly good product to the sale bin. Kate's confectionery packet was a success with the customers but the retailers hated it because it took up so much space and in the end the manufacturer was forced to drop it.

Product safety is also a factor that Kate has to consider. 'Certain products have to be child- and idiot-proof,' she says, 'and that is not necessarily the same thing. There have also been food-tampering scares, so some products have to be made secure from any kind of deliberate or accidental contamination.'

The first step that Kate has to take is a meeting with the product and brand managers, to discuss the packaging concept. 'They often have an existing package that they want to update and modernise but still keep the recognisable look and feel.' The priorities, such as brand development, product protection and the extent to which the packaging will be a sales tool, are discussed and established. 'I then have certain factors and limitations, like the physical size of the product, that I have to work around. Then I have to think about delivery and distribution – will the packages need to be packed into larger boxes? The size, shape, materials, colour and text are all important issues which have to be brought together into the packaging design,' says Kate.

She usually has to design several versions of a new package and then let the marketing manager of the client company make the final choice. 'They often do some field market testing with the different packages to see what the public thinks of each. That is a very nerve-racking time for me, in case they say that they don't like any of my suggestions!'

Kate has to work closely with the market research

professionals, constantly checking whether packet design continues to complement the brand objectives. 'In my job I have to work with a lot of other people, so I need the creative skills and the people skills.' The design is done largely on computers, so she has to understand an assortment of software and networking programmes. 'I'm not technical,' she says, 'but I know how to get the computer to do what I want it to do. As soon as anything goes wrong I call in the technical support specialists.'

Getting the package right can be a high-risk enterprise, says Kate, and some excellent products have sunk without trace because the packaging was wrong. 'I like the job because it involves complex decisions, high cost and high risk, as well as a high level of creative juice.'

Kate has already been offered a job as a product manager in-house with one of her agency's clients, because of her creative and people skills, but she says that she enjoys the level of responsibility she has already and doesn't want more. 'My job is very hands-on and I can see the results.'

Skills you'll need

- Technical ability, to be able to work with computer-aided design software and send images electronically. But Kate says, 'I have a user's knowledge of IT, not a support manager's knowledge. If I get into trouble, there is always someone to sort it out. I know the main functions and commands – that's all anyone needs.'
- Design skills, obviously, to basic BTEC (Business and Technician Education Council) if not degree level. But experience can count for more than endless qualifications in the real world.
- Marketing awareness and the willingness to study marketing theory further. Eventually, you should consider doing a sales and marketing course with the Chartered Institute of Marketing (CIM).
- Enthusiasm, reliability and the ability to focus on short- and long-term objectives need to be blended with creative and people skills. You'll spend some time in meetings as well as designing and the designs have to conform to parameters set by others.

Tips

- You'll probably be doing art A level, but try to specialise in graphics whenever you can.
- Try to get into the habit of evaluating products as you buy them. What makes *you* choose one product over another, when the package's contents are probably fairly similar? Will you ever pay more for a certain type of package?

How to get into Marketing and PR

Photographer

Money: As a staff photographer expect around £18,000, but if you're prepared to go freelance you could expect to be earning £30,000 within six months.

Hours: As a creative worker you'll often start late and stay late, but you'll have to attend marketing, creative and client meetings, which are often held in normal business hours.

Health risk: Low, although some of the equipment and lighting is heavy and awkward.

Pressure rating: Medium to high. One problem is that you'll create shots which you love but the client says are awful.

Glamour rating: High. Since the likes of David Bailey first glamourised the job, and because many photographers are high-profile creative people, the image of the photographer has been enviable.

Travel rating: Medium to high. Depending on the client and the campaign, there may be travel to exotic locations anywhere in the world. Or you may be stuck in a basement studio or darkroom for weeks on end. There will also be meetings with clients, which are often held at their offices or at the marketing consultancy.

The marketing industry has always been a rich source of revenue for photographers – most marketing strategies involve visual images. However, you need to be innovative to take the pictures that will set one campaign above another and create images that are instantly associated with certain brands and products.

Claire Owen wanted to be a photographer ever since she picked up a camera at school and took a short media studies taster course in Year 10. She says, 'I just love taking pictures and really like pictures of people more than anything else.' Despite that, Claire has now made her name as a food photographer, taking still pictures for the packaging on food products. She continues, 'There are so many tricks in this trade, I couldn't possibly tell you all of them. But I have also developed a few tricks of my own, which I certainly wouldn't tell anyone.'

Claire's career has not always been straightforward and although she earns good money now it hasn't always been easy. She says, 'I did a graphic design course after media studies A level, but have always specialised in photography. I tried to go freelance after leaving college but found it very hard.'

As a freelancer she had to 'sell' herself and negotiate with commissioning art editors and marketing executives, as well as taking the pictures. Without much experience and with no name or reputation, just getting work was very difficult. 'There are literally hundreds of freelance photographers out there and it was just terribly hard to even get someone to look at my portfolio.'

Eventually Claire gave up on being a freelancer for the time being. 'I realised that you need a body of published work and lots of contacts and you don't just leave college and announce that you are a freelance, at least, not without some way of earning a living while you build up the work.'

She got a job with a marketing consultancy as the in-house photographer after starting as a junior in the art department. 'It was a fluke really. They didn't even have a job as an in-house photographer and when I started I was just doing basic design and layout tasks and being a "gofer" for everyone else on the art and design team.' But one day there was a job which needed photography and the regular freelancer was booked elsewhere. 'I said I'd do it, they were pleased with the results and I haven't looked back since then,' Claire says.

Now she is involved in the initial creative meetings with the clients, when ideas are outlined and visualisations expressed. 'You learn to interpret what clients say. For example, they say they want a young look and that's all in the lighting and colours.' She has a studio within the consultancy, although she is now thinking of building her own and having another go at being freelance. 'There's no doubt that I'd earn twice as much as a freelance and now that I have a good portfolio of product shots and magazine layouts, it shouldn't be too hard to get going.'

Claire is also planning to hire an agent, who will take 15 per cent of her fees but will arrange all the bookings and do the business management, like sending out bills to clients and chasing payment. 'I hate that side of things and I'm no good at it, so I'd rather concentrate on taking pictures and earning money and pay someone else to do the office donkey work.'

Working for a consultancy has given Claire the chance to use some of the latest digital technology. 'Some is quite expensive,' she says, 'and I have been able to try out and learn to use some of the latest products and technologies without investing in them myself.' She is going to have to buy digital equipment as well as conventional cameras when she turns freelance, but says that she will be getting a business loan to start her off. 'There will also be a period when I won't be receiving any money, when I first start working. In fact, it may be many months before the actual income I receive builds up to a living wage.' Claire has talked it all through with the small business adviser from her bank and understands now about cash flow and the importance of selling herself.

She says that she will miss life in the consultancy, though. 'It's great being part of a team and having the "coffee-machine chats" each day, just chit-chatting about what was on TV last night and stuff like that. As a freelance you are on your own far more and I shall miss everyone that I work with.' She is hoping, though, that the consultancy will continue to use her as one of its preferred photographers when she takes the freelance plunge. 'It will be nice to keep working with these people and with clients that I know.'

Skills you'll need

■ Photographers have to take a verbal or written brief and turn it into something visually stunning. That is a very particular skill, although Claire says it is something that can be learned. 'You tune in to what people are getting at when they describe what they are imagining as a finished image. I have to be able to interpret their ideas and turn them into eye-catching images which flatter and match the brand and appeal to the target market.'

■ Technology skills are almost as important as a basic knowledge of photography. Digital cameras are standard these days and the photographer has to know how to send images electronically. Images are used on websites and the photographer has to know the practical limits for downloading image files. Claire says, 'I have to think when I'm taking a picture of where it will be used, such as on a billboard, on packaging, on promotional literature, in a magazine or on a website. When I am photographing food, for example, I have to know which tricks to use depending on how the image is going to be used.'

Tips

■ Photographers have always – rightly or wrongly, probably wrongly – been judged by their sense of style as much as by their creative output. Clothes and style are crucial for their credibility. Don't even think about a navy blazer with brass buttons, unless by the time you read this that's the latest ironic fashion. A keen fashion sense, whatever the prevailing fashion, is essential.

■ Stay smart, even if that means casual. Photographers, like other creative people, can dress down, but that is not a licence to let it all hang out. Don't have ungroomed toes in sandals, for example; don't even think about shorts in a business office; avoid your navel or cleavage showing, no matter how gorgeous you look. However casually you dress, there are always limits that separate the business environment from playtime. If you want to be respected, don't go beyond the limits for your age or body shape. Be outrageous, be interesting, but don't be offensive.

Point-of-sale merchandiser

Money: Medium. You're likely to start on £15,000 as a graduate but could see your salary rise to £22,000. More responsibility may see it go up to £35,000. There may be a few perks, depending on the client.

Hours: Mixed. Likely to start on the basic 10–6 but you may have to work overtime.

Health risk: Low. You're unlikely to have to carry and put up the displays yourself.

Pressure rating: Medium. Depending on your seniority, you will have varying levels of responsibility for the point of sale, which is often an essential component of an overall advertising or promotion campaign. So if you get it wrong, you will be letting a lot of other people down.

Glamour rating: Low to medium. Unless you are working on highly innovative promotions, point of sale is not seen as high prestige.

Travel rating: Could be high if you are the one who goes around to every outlet installing the material, but most point-of-sale managers use third parties to undertake the deliveries. The exception is likely to be exhibitions and shows, where the point of sale is so large and such a fundamental element that the presence of the point-of-sale merchandiser will be required.

When you go into a shop or store and see promotional, marketing or advertising material, that is known as marketing merchandise at the point of sale. Obvious, really, but it involves a special arm of marketing which deals with psychology and trends as much as marketing theory and practice.

Sarah Doyle has been working as a point-of-sale merchandiser for a specialist sales promotion agency for three years. She says, 'I did a marketing degree at university so I had some idea of all the different aspects of marketing before I took this job.' She chose to specialise in point-of-sale work because of the combination of skills it needs. 'It has all the elements of a science,' she says, 'but it is also a creative art.' Sarah is called into meetings with the marketing, product and brand managers of her agency's client firm. 'We are a small firm of 30 people and take on all kinds of work which involves point-of-sale merchandising. Sometimes it is part of an advertising campaign, sometimes part of a sales promotion effort. But I always have to consider a balance of look and feel and psychology and bring in my own experience of what works.'

She says that usually she is respected as the expert in her field, largely thanks to her experience. 'We were responsible for a guerrilla point-of-sale campaign which really hijacked the headlines. We had moving holograms in special units alongside the retail counters for a new health product and they were the talking point of the industry for a while.' She explains that they even made the front pages of some of the national newspapers because the technology they used was so advanced. 'It was like the little hologram in *Star Wars* that I remember from my childhood – it was so strange to see the technology that was so advanced then in real use, and I was responsible for the campaign that used it.'

Sarah takes a brief from the client and then spends two or three weeks at most working on the details. 'Then we go back with a proposal, some dummies and a cost.' Then the client decides whether they will accept the proposal or makes their own suggestions which need to be incorporated. 'Usually, the clients accepts the basic concept. I think that is partly because we are able to back up every proposal with a scientific analysis of why it will be successful.'

Among the elements that Sarah has to consider is the **atmosphere** at the point of sale, which can vary from retail point to retail point. 'I have to be able to come up with a generic proposal that will suit many different venues and be equally effective at any time of day and at any location within the store,' she says.

Once the client has accepted, Sarah is responsible for implementing the campaign, which means briefing others within her organisation and using third parties where appropriate. 'We use specialist distribution agents who will physically visit every supermarket, chemist or gift shop in a given area, actually putting up posters, erecting stand-alone units and making sure that they work properly,' she says. This job used to be done by the sales reps but these days the number of reps has dropped as more and more replacement ordering is done electronically with electronic point-of-sale tills which are automatically linked to central stockrooms and wholesalers.

Sarah did a year's postgraduate work on retail psychology, so she understands the thinking processes which govern individuals and groups when they choose, buy and then perhaps also return goods to the store. 'There is no doubt that it is a skilled science,' she says, 'and I also have to understand what makes people switch from one brand to another and how they can divide up one purchase into component parts from different suppliers. There are many variables and many reasons why customers make certain choices.'

Sarah is also involved in a postgraduate project which involves developing electronic point-of-sale devices. 'The customer goes to a booth and can surf for information. We can extract as much about the customer as possible which we can use in future and the customer has the option to make a purchase,' she explains. In an estate agent, booths are used to show videos of properties for sale; in holiday shops, to show locations and hotel rooms; and in airports, the booths are used to book cars at destination locations or hotel rooms and to order other goods. 'I am using my retail experience to develop new technologies at the point of sale,' Sarah says.

In some stores, the booths use video disks, but most today are web enabled and connected to the Internet, so that the link between customers and manufacturers or suppliers can be more immediate and personal. 'There has never been much customer resistance to point-of-purchase booths,' says Sarah. 'Any fears about security are allayed because they don't have to give their credit card numbers over the machines. These are given to the person in the store. It is an effective combination of human and IT interface which reassures customers and encourages them to buy.'

Every campaign ends with a post-event appraisal, for which Sarah has to produce another report. 'There is a fair amount of report reading and writing,' she says, 'but most of the job is thinking up original ideas and making them happen.'

WAP technology is also revolutionising point-of-sale merchandising. Sarah says, 'I have to be able to understand technologies like wireless application protocol and **Bluetooth**, which enable applications to be complex and innovative. We can give our customers a unique merchandising campaign which really sets them apart from their competitors – that is my objective.'

As well as understanding customers and the psychology of purchasing, Sarah has to be able to come up with different solutions for completely different retail environments. 'One day I'm working on a point-of-sale strategy for garages, another day it will be discount stores. Then it might be a chain of prestigious supermarkets, then airports. Each one has different elements, a different customer mindset and a different physical environment which will cause more or less stress on the point-of-sale material,' she says.

Sarah has to work with the creative team, including artists and photographers, as well as the people who make up the units and the distributors. 'I brief the creatives and want them to come up with something eye-catching but not off-putting. Often I am trying to get people to switch from one brand to another or to try a completely new product. Sometimes I have to answer consumers' questions and need to predict and anticipate what they will want to know, other times I have to provide units which will close transactions or provide after-sales service contacts for customers. Everything I do is aimed at enhancing the brand and building on the brand values, so those have to be taken into account in the initial proposal and in the execution.'

Sometimes Sarah works as part of a far larger marketing or launch team and in these instances doesn't have to think of catchlines or slogans. On other projects she does and she will have brainstorming sessions when ideas are worked through, project timelines set and third parties commissioned and briefed. 'I love the variety,' she says, 'and I like the responsibility. It's up to me whether a campaign works or not, and I like to be known for initiating the most interesting, innovative and successful campaigns in the area of point of sale.'

Skills you'll need

- Point-of-sale work is a complex combination of the creative, the psychological and the organisational. Sarah has to devise the original concept and sell it to the client and then see the campaign through to the final review. She says, 'A good degree in some course which requires determination and analysis is essential.'
- Technology is important and so is the ability to understand the potential and limitations of new technologies such as WAP as they are developed. 'I have to work closely with technical people and have to be able to talk their jargon,' Sarah says.
- Languages are useful, if not vital. Sarah explains, 'I speak business French and German and find that I often have to use them.' She often works with European marketing, brand and product managers on pan-European campaigns. She also understands the different purchasing psychologies in other European countries. 'I'd like to extend that to studying global purchasing psychology, so I know what makes customers in Japan buy things and what influences them at point of sale. Australia and China, South America and India – all cultures have different values and different views of trade shows, giveaways, demonstrations and other selling opportunities and efforts.'

■ Start by taking notice of existing and new point-of-sale campaigns. See the devices they use to catch the customers' attention. What makes you take notice and what makes you buy? What actually influences your decision-making? Only by putting yourself in the shoes of the customer, by being that customer, can you be an effective point-of-sale merchandiser.

Glossary

■ **Atmosphere**
The total of the physical characteristics of a retail store or a group of stores, including their routes to the consumer, such as the Internet, used to develop an image and attract customers.

■ **Bluetooth**
An electronic communications standard which allows for wireless connection between devices and peripherals in a small area. So within an office, a couple of PCs might share a printer and modem using Bluetooth.

■ **WAP technology**
Wireless application protocol, likely to be the biggest leap in communications since the advent of the mobile phone. It allows individuals to log onto the Internet from any location, using their mobile or desktop PC, accessing data that may be personally tailored.

PR assistant

Money: Poor. You might only get £8,000 on starting, but expect it to rise fast to around £13,000 or £15,000. Not many perks, apart from clients' products. If the client is a car manufacturer, you can't expect a car yet, though.

Hours: Usually regular except when there's a crisis on and then you'll be expected to work as hard as everyone else.

Health risk: Telephoning journalists can be a health risk, but otherwise it's office work and there's not much risk apart from photocopier fumes.

Pressure rating: Low, unless you are taking the job and your prospects seriously, in which case medium.

Glamour rating: Depends on the client, but can be good. Schmoozing with journalists could be glamorous to some.

Travel rating: Low unless you count trips to exhibition centres or to the printers to pick up some brochures.

When you first start in PR, this is likely to be your job title. It is interchangeable with 'dogsbody' and 'junior' because you will be asked to do all the boring menial tasks. But this is how you learn, so tackle them cheerfully and willingly, keep your eyes and ears open and you'll soon progress.

Your job specification as a PR assistant depends on the size of the agency, consultancy or in-house department, but you can be fairly sure that it is labour intensive, boring and without much apparent importance. Don't be misled. People will be watching how you conduct yourself, how efficiently and charmingly you complete even the most mundane task, so give everything you do your best effort.

Don't regard it as being a junior, think of it as an opportunity that is interesting and educational. Before you know it, you'll be able to apply for jobs with labels like PR executive, PR manager or even, ultimately, PR director. All offer more money and greater responsibility, but everyone in these roles starts as a PR assistant.

Kristen Lake has been a PR assistant for nine months since leaving university. She says, 'There is invariably a lot of tea and coffee making. You'll have to set up meetings, book meeting rooms, inform everyone that there is a meeting and then remind them again the day or hour before. You'll be expected to take notes during the meeting and produce a report and circulate it afterwards, with indications of who is expected to do what before the next meeting. This is a junior job, but if you keep your eyes and ears open you can learn a lot, fast.'

Simon Lattimer is managing director of a PR agency and advises, 'You should start compiling your own personal contact book, which you will keep with you through your career. Start making private notes on all the journalists you speak to – these people and your relationship with them are key to your success as a PR professional.' You might be requested to telephone journalists and 'ask them if our press release arrived and whether they are going to use it'. Beware. You're being set up. Journalists are too busy to take this kind of call and no experienced PR professional would dream of making one – but they have no compunction in asking new starters to do so. If you do, you'll find that journalists are frequently brusque. Try to find another reason for the call, if you are forced to ring. Other questions you should never ask a journalist are 'Did you use the comments we sent you?' and 'Do you know when the piece will appear?'

Kristen says, 'You'll probably be asked to check all the key publications and media for each client and cut out all items in which they are mentioned. Hopefully, the mention is positive – if not, the senior PR executives will take steps to manage the client and the journalist in future. Your job will just be to mount the clippings and forward them to the client, on a daily, weekly or monthly basis. Some agencies use a cuttings agency to do this, but many use the internal juniors and assistants.'

You'll be asked to set up filing systems and encourage others in the department to use them. You may be asked to call the advertising departments of magazines and newspapers, requesting forward features lists and media packs. Once the features lists arrive, you'll probably have to check whether there are any features coming up which your clients or managers could contribute to. You may have to check with the journalist writing the piece to see what input they want and then make sure that the client makes contact in good time before the deadline.

One crucial job is keeping the database of magazines and journalists up to date. This means making calls or sending e-mails and, depending on the replies, making amendments to the database files.

If there is promotional activity going on or an exhibition being planned, you can be sure that you will have a busy time – from booking the stand and organising the shell and all the point-of-sale materials to ensuring that everything is where it should be when the exhibition opens, manning the stand, greeting potential customers and trying to get everything done as efficiently as possible for the client. Co-ordinating an exhibition can be a three-month project, with 100 different things to think about and a million things that can go wrong. But get most of it right, be quietly competent and people will notice.

You'll probably have to work with printers and promotional material suppliers, proof-reading brochures and sales material and ensuring that the finished goods are available on time. You might have to order print materials, getting quotes and working to a budget, and making sure that deadlines are met.

A PR assistant's day will probably start with sorting the post and making sure that it is delivered to the right desk. You might have to deal with general enquiries, stuff envelopes and, at the end of the day, do the franking and take everything to the post office.

A major element of PR work is writing press releases, even though most journalists don't read them. But you will probably be asked to write the first draft and trained how to do this. There are plenty of books available on press release writing, but once you get friendly with a couple of journalists you could ask them what releases work best for them. You'll also need to find out how journalists prefer to receive such material, whether by post, fax or e-mail and then make sure that they get it in the preferred way. Nothing annoys a journalist like getting press releases by the wrong delivery method.

If a press event, such as a reception or conference, is being planned, you'll have to prepare the press packs for journalists to take away afterwards. These will include photographs, press releases, case studies and probably some information that is embargoed – hopefully, it won't be published ahead of the time you request. Most journalists will respect an embargo, but it is a gentleman's agreement – not a right that you can demand.

Often the PR assistant has to keep the website updated by keying in new information, so you'll need some basic technical understanding. Don't worry, though – no one will expect too much at first.

Skills you'll need

- An orderly, methodical, structured mind, enabling you to be well organised and conscientious. Foreign languages are helpful – there is often a need to speak to European partners and clients.
- You'll need charm, diplomacy and tact and the ability to mix well with others on the team and with clients.
- Even more than marketing, PR is a communications role and a management function. It is about making sure that the media understand a company's goals and objectives and know about its products and services. You also have to make sure that journalists know that there is a spokesperson or

pundit available. As you get more senior you'll have to answer to the client when they are not quoted in features.

■ Make sure you have basic IT skills so you can use a word processor, a presentation program and e-mail. An understanding of e-mail protocol is also valuable.

Tips

■ If you don't know how to do something you are asked to do, be honest and say so straight away. Better to do that than pretend you know and then get it wrong.

■ Read a book called *Press Here!* (ISBN 0 13 095409 8), which explains the thinking behind journalists' actions and how best to deal with them.

■ Keep a notebook – record everything you are asked to do and the deadline as well as notes, phone numbers, etc.

■ Be careful when speaking to clients and journalists – often they'll ask for the assistant when they want to find out the truth about how something is going, assuming that you won't know enough to cover up or be evasive if necessary. Be charming, but don't tell the client or journalist anything.

■ Unless you are asked for your opinion, keep your own counsel.

■ PR is about managing a reputation – and anything you do can affect the reputation of your company or client.

PR executive / manager

Money:	Could start at £15,000 and reach £60,000 before you've had enough and want to start on your own as a freelancer. Perks depend on the client.
Hours:	Varied. You'll have to do plenty of plod work in routine office hours, but there will be after-hours events, plus schmoozing with journalists and clients in bars and pubs.
Health risk:	Low.
Pressure rating:	Medium to high. Some agencies now offer their staff 'duvet days' which are days off for mental health when the pressure gets too much.
Glamour rating:	Depends on the clients you are handling and the sector you're working in. Can be high, if you are the PR for a top ten pop band, for example, or low if you are working for a toilet-cleaning fluid company.
Travel rating:	Low to medium. The Internet and e-mail have eliminated the need for many face-to-face meetings, but the PR will still have to travel to sit in on meetings between the client and a journalist and to attend trade shows and exhibitions. With luck, you may even have to travel abroad to see clients or attend conferences, but it will usually be the senior PR staff who pick up the jollies and jaunts.

These two terms are often interchangeable and the job specification varies from PR department to agency to consultant. Usually, though, the manager is senior to the executive. Whatever they are called, this is the person responsible for press relations, who has to make sure that the client is mentioned positively in the media. Sometimes the job involves crisis management – dealing with published criticism or misquotes.

Tania Poole has been a PR executive for a year. She says, 'You have to make sure that the ladies and gentlemen of the press know all about the best aspects of your clients' products, services and people. The job is a big, busy and demanding one and involves far more than schmoozing, wining and dining with key journalists. Most of the time is spent in background organisation, planning and chores, some of which can be delegated to the PR assistant.'

She continues, 'You'll have to know the company, its products, services and history inside out and backwards and forwards. Especially, you'll know what historical problems and difficulties the company has experienced and what the outcomes were. You'll have to assume that the journalists know the worst. You'll also have to know who the main competitors are and your own client's unique differentiators. Your objective is to get the journalists to focus on the good news and write favourably about your firm or your clients. Clients regard editorial as free publicity, but there are plenty of hidden costs involved, not least your time.'

Most agencies and consultancies specialise in a market sector, such as **FMCG** or IT. You will also specialise, getting to know the key journalists in that sector, the issues that they want to write about and how your client can be quoted as a pundit.

It will be your responsibility to take a brief from the client or an in-house product manager and work with them on developing a media strategy. You'll have to sell or pitch potential story ideas to editors and journalists, organise press events, write and send out press releases and make sure that maximum positive media coverage is achieved. Tania adds, 'You'll have to pitch for new clients and come up with original ideas and angles for press activity and story ideas.'

Sometimes journalists 'take the PR shilling' and make the transition from one side of the fence to the other. The usual reason is money, because PRs earn far more than journalists. The journalist's skills and understanding of their colleagues' requirements can turn them into excellent PR professionals. They have first-hand knowledge of media requirements and are unlikely to make the sort of gaffes that novice PRs can make. However, it takes a special kind of journalist to make the transition. Journalists are courted, fêted, wined and dined while PRs are treated as a necessary evil.

Historically, journalism has been the preferred route into senior PR positions because of the small pool of suitable people available, but that is changing as PR-specific courses turn out more people with instant media savvy. However, journalists can find it difficult to understand what clients want and to respect the position of the client. A good journalist wants a story in the papers while a good PR may be just as concerned with keeping a story out of the papers. So it is not a suitable career path for every journalist.

Skills you'll need

- Tact, charm and intelligence, without being obsequious, ingratiating or oily. The ability to make the client and journalist think that each is the more important to you and the ability to make each believe that you are being completely honest with them.

- The ability to see a story from the journalist's perspective. Your clients will think that journalists are going to be fascinated by non-stories; your task will be either to turn the story around so that it has a hook or break it gently to the client that there is no story.
- Writing ability. There is so much writing involved in the PR manager's job, from reports to press releases, that there is a special section of the National Union of Journalists (NUJ) dedicated to them.

Tips

- Avoid jargon. Anna Murphy, a PR executive in a mid-sized Bristol-based marketing agency, says, 'Phrases like "the bottom line is" and "at the end of the day" are real turn-offs for marketing professionals and their clients. Most people are wholly underwhelmed by the jargon, so at the end of the day don't bother finding the window of opportunity or try singing from the same hymn sheet. Keep it simple and straightforward.'
- Keep your presentations content-rich and concise. Don't use too much text in your slides. Go for bullet points and soundbites.
- Look smart but be guided by your client. If the client's dress code is for suits, you should wear suits too. Only dress down to match journalists if you are sure that they will appear in smart casual. The PR person should always be dressed slightly more smartly than both client and journalist.

Glossary

- **FMCG**
  Fast-moving consumer goods, which includes products like washing powder and foods.

Press officer

Money: Usually starts at around £15,000 with a ceiling of around £35,000, unless you are the press officer for a giant international corporate. Then you could be making £60,000 or £70,000, plus the usual perks. These vary but can include gym membership, a portable PC for home, pension and healthcare and clients' products.

Hours: Varied, but basically 10–6, the same as the journalists. There may be overtime required if there is a crisis which has to be managed, or evening and lunchtime entertainment of journalists.

Health risk: Low. You might have to carry heavy press releases to the press lounge at an exhibition or trade fair, on behalf of your agency or one of their clients, but otherwise you stand more chance of hurting yourself playing squash with a colleague.

Pressure rating: Medium to high. There is often a drama, crisis or panic of one sort or another. Journalists always want information and comments yesterday or sooner and it is up to you to make sure that they have all the information they need. If they use the wrong facts, your job could be on the line.

Glamour rating: Depends on the agency and its clients, so could be low or high. Any contact with the press is fairly highly regarded.

Travel rating: Medium. Despite the widespread use of e-mail and webcasting there will always be the need for personal contacts whenever journalists are involved.

Like any organisation, including their clients, a marketing agency will have someone appointed to deal with press enquiries. This is the person on the opposite side of the table from the journalist, alongside the in-house PR staff.

When a journalist rings a marketing company to get information about their strategy for growth, for example, or what their clients are planning to spend on a marketing campaign, the call will be handled by the press officer. Sometimes this person is called the PRO or public relations officer – in many firms, press officer and PR person are interchangeable terms for the same job. Adrian Brady, now managing director of a full-service marketing agency, says, 'The press officer is vital for making sure that the journalists get the right story and all the background information they need. It is an important role – if you get it wrong, the journalist will print something like "No one from the firm was available for comment", which is, of course, very damning.'

One journalist says, 'You can often tell a lot about a marketing firm by the way their press officer takes press calls. If they are defensive, I suspect that they have more going on than they want me to know about. If they say they'll send me information and don't I think the whole firm is sloppy. The press officer definitely represents the entire marketing agency or consultancy to the press.'

This need not be a full-time job. A press officer frequently has another job title, that of PR manager. The difference between the two varies according to whom you are speaking to, but generally the press officer role is reactive while that of the PR manager is more proactive. Mark James, who has been in PR for over ten years, says, 'The press officer has to field enquiries from the press and make sure that they get to speak to the right person internally, who can give them the quotes they need. They also have to track publications, write press releases and arrange meetings between marketing executives and the media. These are also part of the job function of the PR officer, but they would also be more dynamic about contacting the journalists in the first place, telling them about stories and generally ensuring that the media has the right spin. They'd positively look for press opportunities, while the press officer is more passive.'

The press officer would be expected to know all about the history of the marketing agency, its clients and their campaigns. There might be a lot to catch up on. Much of the press officer's work, like the PR officer's, would be to fend off hostile enquiries or identify those with a hazardous hidden agenda. Sarah Jones, a press officer with one of the big marketing consultancies, says, 'The journalist might call and appear quite innocent, asking apparently innocuous questions about a client and their marketing campaign and next thing you know there is a big piece in one of the financial papers about how the client is planning to spend so much on publicity, despite poor dividends to shareholders, for example. Journalists are devious and not always how they appear. It's the job of the press officer to know which journalists are dangerous and which can be trusted and make sure they speak to the right person in-house to give them a quote.' It will also be up to the press officer to brief the in-house executive, so that they are aware of the dangers and know what to say. 'It's mainly about research and preparation,' says Jones, 'and having a good relationship with the press.'

Skills you'll need

- Charm and social skills count for more than technical skills, although the ability to send an e-mail and write a press release will stand you in good stead.

- Efficiency and courtesy, especially in the face of hostility and devious intent, could quickly propel you from being an ordinary to an outstanding press officer.

Tips

- Mark says, 'Press officers can't appear to be too defensive or the journalists suspect there is something going on, they have to be helpful without giving anything away. And they have to know all there is to know about the firm, its clients, products and strategies, so they are not wrong-footed by the press.'
- Start a contact book of journalists' names. Try getting to know them, to smooth the paths of communication when they call up and want something. It's much easier to deal with a journalist you know and have had a drink with in the past than one you've never met.
- You have to dress fractionally more smartly than the journalists, but you don't have to wear a suit unless the marketing organisation you represent is very traditional and formal. Smart casual is the most usual garb.

Pricing analyst and / or planner

Money: You'll probably already be a marketing executive or manager before you move into pricing as a speciality. You'll need some experience and qualifications, so the starting salary would be £20,000 with around £50,000 as the ceiling. Perks would be limited, but depend on the product set and the sector you're working in. A software company, for example, might make its latest products available to the marketing team.

Hours: Regular. You're unlikely to have to work late except on very rare occasions.

Health risk: Low. For some, this work might carry a boredom risk, but for the cerebral and strategically minded, it can be satisfying and challenging.

Pressure rating: Medium. If you get the price wrong, the sales will sink and you will get fired. Get it right and you'll be the last to receive thanks.

Glamour rating: Low. Like other back-room workers, you'll be the last to be invited on a jolly or to an exhibition, unless it is to spy on competitors' pricing strategies.

Travel rating: Low to non-existent. You might go to a marketing conference to see the latest IT for pricing marketers, but don't expect much.

One of the variables in a marketing strategy is the price. Get it too low and the company doesn't make optimum profits – get it too high and the products or services will not be competitive and people won't buy. The pricing analyst or pricing planner spends their whole time in the back office, studying statistics, reports and surveys, trying to gauge the right price to achieve the best revenues.

James Hartman, who has been in the marketing industry as a freelance consultant for many years, says, 'The value of a product or service can be both tangible and intangible and both are represented in the price. For example, a tangible value could be the cost saving between your product and a competitor's and an intangible value could be the social prestige that comes from owning a certain product or brand. In the first instance, the price would have to be low enough to make a distinct cost difference and the saving worthwhile. In the second instance, the price could be higher and people will still buy, if the prestige is credible enough.'

In both cases, the price will be linked to the advertising and promotion. For example, an advert for a product which is competing on price will highlight that the price is low and competitive. A product being sold as a prestige item might not mention price at all, but will highlight the social and lifestyle benefits derived from owning it. Pricing is also interlinked with product, distribution and promotional decisions, so anyone responsible for pricing must be able to work with professionals in other marketing disciplines.

Bobby Cameron, who works for a major international research agency, says, 'The job of pricing is specialist but everyone with a marketing title has to know what it means and how to do it. These days marketing departments, agencies and consultancies are having to deconstruct their vertical job definitions and replace them with a flat network of people who are multitalented and that includes pricing skills.'

Anyone undertaking pricing analysis has to be able to read reports and statistics and commission market research and understand the responses. This will increasingly be done electronically, so IT skills are becoming more and more important in pricing work. 'You'll also need to be able to predict supply and demand – there is software to help you do this, but you'll have to know how to use it – so that prices can go up with supply drops or demand increases, when stocks become low,' says James Hartman. 'You have to understand issues like price competition, which happens when there are other sellers also stressing low prices but can lead to such low profits that the margins are too slim to be sustainable, and **non-price competition**, where factors other than price are emphasised.'

You'll have to understand the **Boston Matrix** and product life cycles, because the price of a product can vary from the launch, when prices will be high to attract the status conscious, to further down the line when they are priced to attract the mass market. However, the price cannot be dropped too fast or far or the early purchasers will become disenchanted and disloyal. James says, 'The pricing professional has to understand the psychology of the customer.'

The pricing professional also has to work with the brand manager and the product manager to get the pricing strategy right. He or she has to understand how the brand and product people see the target market and how the goods will compete and sell. James says, 'You have to avoid a me-too strategy, when you just follow others in the market, especially when they are going downwards and eroding margins. Your salary will depend on the product earning enough revenue to pay you.'

Some supermarkets have far cheaper 'own-brand' goods which compete on price and quality with the named brand items. James says, 'Sometimes it is better to take a product out of the market where it is competing on price and relaunch it on non-price values. That's where the branding, image and promotion come in.'

Products are sometimes marketed as 'loss leaders', which means that they are ticketed at below cost just to attract customers, in the hope that you can switch-sell other products with better margins or develop loyalty to a brand. James says, 'There is a degree of strategy in costing and cunning in pricing, which makes the job attractive to people who play chess, for example, or like other strategic games.'

Being a pricing professional may mean that you don't meet customers or clients, except occasionally. This is a back-room job for someone interested in marketing but less keen on the social interaction that many find so attractive in marketing careers. James says, 'The pricing analyst can spend all their time reading and writing reports, making recommendations and building strategies. Of all the jobs in marketing, this is one of the more cerebral, but very interesting if you are that way inclined.'

Skills you'll need

- Intelligent analytical abilities are essential, although anyone with a degree in any discipline should be able to pick up these specific skills.
- There are laws affecting pricing which you should be aware of, such as legislation against price fixing and cartels.

Tips

- If pricing interests you, learn some of the terms like 'pricing elasticity', 'unitary demand', 'subjective price' and 'horizontal price fixing'. Start dropping them into your everyday conversation – see how comfortable you feel with the jargon.

Glossary

- **Boston Matrix**
  A theory developed by the Boston Consulting Group which categorises products according to their stage in their life cycle. Products are called either falling stars, cash cows, problem children or rising stars, with a strategy for marketing, pricing and promotion for each.
- **Non-price competition**
  When the role of price in competition is reduced and the emphasis is on other factors, like packaging, delivery, availability or service.

Print manager

Money: Depends on experience and the size of the organisation you work for, but probably starting at £16,000 and reaching £30,000. A senior print manager with responsibility for setting budgets and able to deal with the most difficult printers could probably command £40,000.

Hours: Fairly regular 10–6, but printers do a lot of their business in the pub after work and you'll have to be able to work in that environment.

Health risk: Low, although the boozy, laddish after-work culture can take its toll.

Pressure rating: Medium to high. A lot of what you are responsible for is out of your hands and that can be highly stressful.

Glamour rating: Low. This is a behind-the-scenes but crucial job. Don't expect recognition from the client or even the marketing manager, despite the fact that if the print manager is inefficient a whole campaign can fail.

Travel rating: Low to medium. You might have to travel to the printers or occasionally to the client if you are a senior print manager, but mainly you'll be deskbound and working electronically.

The Internet has reduced the number of forests that marketing teams routinely fell to produce all the documents and reports they commission, but there is still a big need for point-of-sale literature, sales specification brochures, promotional materials and advertising billboards. The variety is almost limitless. The print manager is responsible for liaising with the printers to make sure all print requirements are produced on time and to brief. There is plenty that can go wrong, so those who do this job need to be conscientious and able to work to a deadline.

Being print manager is a production management job, says Zoe Bates, who started as a junior production assistant in a magazine publishing house immediately after leaving university. She says, 'I had a holiday job there and when I finished university they were happy to take me on as a junior learning all about print and production. I did media studies at university and at one time wanted to be a journalist, but then I realised that I preferred the structured, organised production side.'

With the publishing house she learned all about print and how to work with printers, who are a unique group in terms of their jargon and ways of working. 'Most printers are men and it is a very male-oriented world,' she says. On the magazine she had to liaise with editorial and advertising production, which she says drove her mad and was the reason why she moved to a marketing agency. 'At least I only have one set of bosses now, whereas in the publishing house I was working for two completely different sets of people. Now I have just one marketing team, although of course I also have to deal with the clients sometimes.'

Zoe usually gets involved in the strategies once they have been approved and signed off. Her boss is also involved at the early planning stage and sets the print budgets, which are part of the initial costings. 'I go to the marketing managers and sometimes the product and brand managers within the client organisations and basically find out what they want. Then I define it in a print order, talk it through with the printers, work with the designers to make sure all the computer files are ready and make sure that the files get to the printers from the designers and copywriters in time.'

Zoe's work is highly deadline driven. She makes sure that every aspect of a job is properly signed off, with a purchase order and a budget to cover it, but she is not responsible for setting the budgets. 'I have to chase people. Either I am chasing the photographers or the copywriters or the art designers, to make sure that they do their part on time to meet the schedule when the work has to reach the printers. They have strict print slots allocated to each job and we can't be late.'

Then she has to make sure that the printers deliver the finished work on time. 'It's amazing how many jobs get lost or how many jobs, no matter how they are signed off with the files sealed, seem to get gremlins in them with mistakes appearing by the time the final work is produced.' Zoe is responsible for proof-reading the final work against the original files sent by the copywriters and designers. 'Occasionally a mistake is made in the original file, but more often the printers have somehow managed to introduce an error. Don't ask me how. They always shrug their shoulders and say it's not their fault, but it is my job to make sure that any mistake is rectified and the printer doesn't try to charge us if it was their fault.'

She says she likes working with printers. 'They are a weird and wonderful bunch. I compare them with market traders. They are often salt of the earth, although they can be grumpy and very crude sometimes. But they are almost always also gentlemen and they like seeing me around. That's what they say, anyway.'

Most of Zoe's knowledge has been picked up on the job and at her previous job with the publishing house. 'There is an awful lot to learn,' she says, 'and most of it is quite technical.' She has been on a couple of IT courses recently and now understands better how the technology works. 'Most work comes in electronically these days,' she says, 'and I have to download and check it before it goes on to the printers. That way, they can't blame us or say that files were incomplete.'

Once the jobs are printed Zoe also has to keep tabs on the work, making sure she knows where it is stored and getting it to the locations where it is needed.

New technologies are being introduced all the time. 'There are fashions and new trends in print just like anything else and because I work for a marketing agency, of course, the managers want the latest print fashions available for their clients. I go one step farther and make sure that I know the latest things the printers are working on and show them to the marketing managers so they know what they can include in their next campaign.' Zoe also has to be able to supply prices for the different new techniques, so that the marketing managers can cost them and price them into the budgets.

Skills you'll need

- Good English and maths – the English for checking final proofs and finished printwork, the maths for working out and checking various aspects of the print, like volumes and sizes.
- You'll also have to be a strong character, able to work with marketing managers who always want their print yesterday and the printers who will swear blind that the problem couldn't have been their mistake. The print manager is caught between the two and has to ensure that everything flows smoothly when circumstances always seem to conspire against this. Zoe says, 'At times you have to be charming, other times tough and almost aggressive. You have to be flexible and willing to work hard when there is a need.'
- Budgets and deadlines are crucial and the print manager has to work with enthusiasm even on boring projects like pricing schedules or detailed product catalogues. Zoe says, 'Sometimes the subject matter is really interesting but by the time you've seen it through the process you are sick of it. The real interest has to be the production process, and working with print.'
- You'll need IT skills as well as interpersonal skills, but mainly the job requires the ability to stick to a deadline and make sure that everyone else does too.
- You'll have to be flexible and adaptable, able to switch between jobs and keep 100 different things in your head.

Tips

- Even while still at school you can start by learning some of the different terms and the print techniques. Take every opportunity to study print colours and to learn the software that designers and printers use.

Product manager

Money: Can be good. To reach product manager level you'll need to spend several years in sales or marketing or in both and you'll probably be in your late twenties before you get to be a full product manager rather than an assistant. You could start on £25,000 but this could reach £70,000 if you are good and have a clutch of high-profile, prestigious products to look after.

Hours: Basically 10–6, routine office hours, but you can be sure that there will be times when you have to work overtime and at weekends. If you have to work overtime too often, you are either not very good at the job or your employer has given you too much for one person to do.

Health risk: Low. Unless you are product manager of high-performance cars, which need constant road-testing, there is not much danger to your health or safety.

Pressure rating: Medium to high. You have ultimate responsibility for the success of a product, and if you do the job well, use a good team and are a good team player and manager, there shouldn't be too much pressure. But if your products are becoming increasingly unfashionable, the market is shrinking and production costs keep going up, you could be for the high jump and the pressure will be on.

Glamour rating: Depends on the products or services you are responsible for. If it is a brand of ice cream, there's not a lot of glamour, but if you work for a hi-tech company with some sexy products or in the media in some way, you could find yourself on the glamour fast track.

Travel rating: Varies. It depends on where the products are made and the location of the various people you need to work with and whose activities you have to co-ordinate, but with the rise of e-mail and webcam desktop video conferencing, the occasions on which you'll have to travel to meetings will be few and far between. That said, you might have to travel to international conferences and go to press launches of your new products or travel abroad to see what your competitors are up to.

The product manager's role is a hybrid sales and marketing one, with responsibility for improving sales through marketing. Other marketing jobs are usually less tightly tied to sales results than this one. The product manager has ultimate responsibility for how well a product or group of products does and that is judged by the 'bottom line' or profit margin.

The responsibilities of product managers vary wildly from company to company and may even differ within one firm. They depend on the product or service sector, the size of the market and the department, and can be almost entirely sales oriented or, at the other end of the spectrum, almost entirely strategic. No two product managers have the same job, but what they have in common is a sense of 'ownership' of the product or service.

Deborah Rich is product manager for a large computer manufacturing company, responsible for a group of PC and desktop products. She says, 'I have to understand and translate customer desires into product development or modification, work with the marketing manager on communication, promotions and advertising campaigns and with the sales manager on sales strategies.' She explains that sometimes she feels like the hub of a wheel. 'I have to work with several other people who have specific tasks, the spokes of the wheel, while I am in the middle pulling everything together.' The difficulty comes from the fact that Deborah has no direct control over the other departments, but is responsible for their efforts.

Yet she says that she likes the power and influence that her job offers. 'It can be very rewarding. I have the authority to make the decisions that will determine the success of the product set that I am responsible for. I have autonomy to work independently and, although I am responsible to the sales director and the board, I have the freedom to do virtually what I want to achieve my objectives. I feel that I am my own boss.' The job is also a considerable intellectual challenge, she says. 'I have to analyse markets, plot a brand's direction and get inside the mind of the buyer. In the IT market, and particularly the PC market, this is dynamic and fascinating.

'I also have to track what our competitors are doing, watching their pricing strategies and promotional activity and make sure that we are not wrong-footed. It's like a chess game, constantly trying to stay three moves ahead.'

There is a high degree of confidentiality in Deborah's work. She knows what the research and development teams are working on, even before they start work. She is planning the pricing and the marketing strategies while the products are in development and by the time they go into production she is ready to launch them on the unsuspecting world. She says, 'Sometimes I'll work on a secret new product and at the last minute find that one of our competitors has something very similar. Then I have to try to find some other point or differential on which we can promote and sell it.'

Deborah works extensively with third parties, such as a market research agency, a PR agency and a marketing and creative design agency. She has relationships with each group and sometimes brings them all together for meetings and to decide cohesive strategies. 'At least the firm I work for is based entirely in the UK,' she says. 'I have a friend who works for an American firm in a similar role and she has to go to the States for meetings about once a month. It sounds fun, but it gets boring and tiring after a while. I'd rather be based in the UK – I still get plenty of chance to travel.'

Best of all, says Deborah, is the variety of the job. 'I never know what each day will bring.' There is a combination of human resource planning, hard data commissioning and analysis, production, sales, finance and media relations work. 'In a single day I can have meetings with loads of different people. Then I've got to read and write reports and still find time just to think about what needs to be done. It's busy and demanding, but it's great fun.' It is an exciting and fulfilling career, says Deborah, for those who like a challenge and working with people.

Skills you'll need

- You must be a team player, able to work with others of completely different dispositions, agendas and personalities. Deborah says, 'Salespeople can be quite different from creative marketing types and the product manager has to be able to fit in easily with both.' You'll have to be able to set up and run meetings, ensuring that everyone has their say while you get what you want without upsetting anyone.
- You must be creative and good at planning. You'll have to work with the marketing and design teams, thinking through new packaging, promotional and sales materials, and with the sales team to plan the sales strategies and targets for the next year or even further ahead.
- You have to be reliable and able to take responsibility. Being product manager involves plenty of routine general management tasks, which you consistently have to take the initiative in establishing and implementing. This is an action job.
- You must be a self-starter, able to initiate activity and inspire creativity in others. You'll have to set targets and objectives for yourself and others, manage projects, set milestones and penalties, check and recheck that everything is happening to schedule, and ensure success. Failure is not a concept that product managers are allowed to consider.

Tips

- Courses in the sciences, maths and economics help develop the problem-solving and strategic logic skills that you will need.
- You'll have to be a team leader, so practise taking the initiative and working without supervision. All these skills can be developed during GCSE and A level work.

Production manager

Money: Medium. A junior production assistant might start on £13,000 or £14,000, but by the time you have several years' experience and know how to make sure that all the elements of a marketing campaign are in place at the right time, you could command £35,000 or £40,000. In a big agency with several clients, an efficient production manager can save the firm lots of money by looking for economies of scale, co-ordinating the elements of projects for several clients, and salaries can reach £60,000. There are sometimes perks from the printers which can be valuable.

Hours: Routine. There may be some overtime but that depends on levels of staffing and your efficiency. A good production manager will be so well organised that overtime will be unnecessary.

Health risk: Low.

Pressure rating: Medium to high. You will have to cope with the stress of being dependent for your success on the reliability of others, which can be highly stressful. But the more efficient you are, the lower the overall pressure.

Glamour rating: Low. As with many back-room jobs, people often have no idea what a production manager does or how important the role is to the overall campaign.

Travel rating: Low. Most of the work will be at your own desk. Even when it becomes necessary to chase others for work which threatens to miss the deadline, most of the contact will be by telephone or e-mail.

Like the print manager, the production manager has to liaise with different departments and co-ordinate jobs. But in the production manager's role there are far more elements to think about than just the printers and the marketing manager or client.

Anyone thinking of becoming a production manager must be unflappable under pressure and able to keep ten dozen different things in the air at once, according to Jason Beck, who works as a production manager for a top London marketing consultancy. 'My job is to make sure that everything is in place for the campaign to happen and then at all stages as the campaign unfolds,' he says, 'and I have to work between lots of different people co-ordinating everything.'

Every campaign is different, explains Jason. 'Last month we did a sales promotion campaign for a car company and I had to make sure that every car dealership in the country had all the point-of-sale material and posters that they needed to support the advertising which was going out simultaneously on TV and at cinemas.'

In many ways Jason's job is similar to that of a project manager (see *Project or campaign manager*) but with a slightly narrower remit. 'The project manager has to make sure that all the conceptual stages are followed through, while my task is, like the print manager, more focused on the execution of a campaign,' he explains.

The production manager usually uses project management tools, often software, which ensures that he remembers to do everything at the right stage. There are critical cut-off times after which it would be too late to order print, for example, or commission artwork. 'The stages of a campaign are fairly well defined,' says Jason, 'but they have to be in order.' If there is a project manager in overall charge of several projects, the production manager will report to him or her. In the absence of a project manager, it will be left to the production manager to make sure that all the details are taken care of.

'I often have 25 or 30 different campaigns on the go at any one time,' says Jason. 'And they will all be at different stages.' There is a project manager at the consultancy where Jason works, so he doesn't have to think too much about getting the campaigns in the right order or ensuring economy of scale on certain tasks by running jobs together. 'My job is just to make sure that everything happens when it is supposed to,' he says.

He likes the variety of the job. 'My work crosses all the internal departments and pulls together many different clients. I'll find myself working with the creative and art team one day and the print production and distribution team the next. Then I'll work with the advertising creatives and with the billboard site bookers the next. I have to make sure that if there is a glitch or hold-up in one section it doesn't affect all the others. My main nightmare is a domino effect which results in a campaign running late for some reason.' If the posters for a billboard campaign are held up and the campaign does not run until after the product launch, obviously impact and hence sales are affected.

In many firms, particularly small ones, the print management and production management jobs are combined. 'Until recently I had to take care of print production as part of my job,' says Jason, 'but then there were so many print jobs coming through that there was enough for a separate job and they hired an efficient junior to do the print management side. Now I have overall control of all production and report to the project manager, who also works more on the client side. I don't have much to do with clients at all.'

The division of responsibility changes considerably from agency to agency and consultancy to consultancy, depending on how many there are in the production team. In a medium-sized agency, it is possible that all the print, production and project management jobs are rolled together. Even in enterprises where there are several in the department, they may be split according to job responsibility, or by client. In the latter case, one person will be responsible for seeing through all the print and production for each client, a system which offers the benefit of a single person having overall responsibility. 'That's the way I work with my two colleagues,' says Jason. 'I am involved with each client project and see it through from first planning and approval to post-event post mortem. That way, if something goes wrong, I have to carry the can regardless of at which stage the problem arose.'

Jason likes the job because although there is a lot of responsibility there is not much risk-taking involved. 'Basically, I do what others tell me and just make sure that everything happens on time,' he says. 'Each job has a strict schedule and set of deadlines which I have to watch, making sure that every element happens when it is supposed to.'

If anyone falls behind, it is Jason's job to spot their tardiness and do something about it. 'I have to crack the whip and sort out problems,' he says. 'I have to make sure that others respect me and will do what I ask.'

Jason does not have to think up or communicate creative ideas, like the marketing manager. 'I'm like a back-up person, making sure that all the mechanics are working and in place so that the creative and sales teams can sell their ideas, confident in the knowledge that they will be put efficiently into action,' he says.

Jason does not have to be a leader, either, which suits him. As a senior production manager he has areas he specialises in, and certain of the agency's clients for whom he has responsibility, and although there are junior people in the team, none reports to him. 'I like to think I am a good team player but I don't like having people working for me,' he says.

Skills you'll need

- Your organisational skills obviously have to be first-rate, enabling you to set targets and plan and manage a series of events and to make sure that everyone involved sticks to the deadlines. Invariably, there will be some who won't, so the ability to charm and persuade is highly desirable.
- Basic computing skills are necessary. Programming ability is unnecessary, but you must be able to create project files, send

and receive e-mails and ensure that picture and document files are sent from department to department and to third parties.

- People who like safety and working within defined parameters often like being production managers. Although the ability to use initiative is required, you also have to like working to preset deadlines and processes.
- A sense of urgency and commitment and an awareness of the importance of deadlines and timeliness are fairly crucial. And although this is a back-office job, you need an awareness of the clients and their importance.
- Production managers need to be flexible and adaptable where necessary. Sometimes things don't happen according to plan and the manager has to be able to seek and implement alternatives so that the end objective is still achieved on time.

Tips

- Being a production manager is an organisational and management job, so while still at school seek out any opportunity to organise and manage your schoolfriends and family!
- Practise setting timelines and deadlines by working out how long certain tasks take, looking at how a complete job can be broken into component parts and seeing how each component can be speeded up to improve the overall job.

Project or campaign manager

Money: Depending on seniority and the number of projects or campaigns you handle, can be from £18,000 to £35,000 or even £40,000. In a major agency, the campaign manager is crucial in ensuring the smooth execution of campaigns and reducing costs – that role is not underestimated and the responsibility is reflected in the salary. In other agencies the job is just given back-room status and is not particularly well rewarded. The perks depend on the clients you handle, but you'll probably get fewer than the marketing manager, who has front-line contact with the client. As a senior campaign manager with several years' experience you'll get some company perks like health insurance, gym membership and possibly a fleet car.

Hours: If you are well organised you can probably get away with routine 10–6, but there will inevitably be times when things seem to be going pear-shaped and it will be up to you to sort them out. Then you will be expected to work as much overtime as is required.

Health risk: Low.

Pressure rating: Medium to high. You'll be depending on other people to get their part right, and any job that depends on others to that degree is bound to be stressful. But if you are well organised you can reduce that stress to as low a level as possible.

Glamour rating: Low. As with all back-room jobs with low levels of client contact, there is not much prestige attached to this one.

Travel rating: Low to medium. You will do most of your work from your desk, communicating with all the parties involved in a project by telephone and e-mail, but there will be times when you have to visit third parties, sites and so forth.

Most marketing managers have overall campaign responsibility, but in really large consultancies, agencies or enterprises, a separate campaign or project manager leaves the creative work to the marketing, product and brand managers and takes care of the operational tasks. This role may be called campaign manager in other firms, with exactly the same responsibilities.

Josh Blackwell started his career as a marketing manager and ended up specialising in the operational side. He says, 'I just wasn't very good at the creative side and I didn't like the meetings with the clients. I'm much better at managing all the elements and processes which go together to make a whole campaign.'

Josh is involved right from the start, at the conceptual stage, even before the client has accepted and signed off a job. 'I'm needed to make sure that they think of everything, that everything is included in the costings and to make sure that the timings are in the right order.' However, Josh rarely goes along to client meetings. 'That suits me,' he says. 'I like to be a back-room person. I can't stand having to deal with clients. All that smarming and charming – I hate it.'

Once a client has approved a campaign, the marketing manager delegates all the operational work to Josh. 'I just take it away and make sure it happens,' he says. His first job is to take another long look at the plan and make sure that everything has been thought of. 'I put every job into a computer software program which helps allocate costs to each element of the campaign. So that my time, for example, is charged to whichever client's job I'm working on at any time. It also logs all the incidental costs and materials, as well as the charges from outside third parties.' The software also helps manage the life of the project and ensures that certain tasks are completed on time. 'It alerts me if something hasn't been completed,' says Josh. 'And it can automatically send out reminders to other people if they haven't completed a task by a predetermined time.'

As much of Josh's time is spent making sure that everyone involved in each project is properly briefed as it is chasing people. 'If everyone is professional and competent, and most people are, then the need to chase and hustle is kept to a minimum. If I've briefed them properly and made sure that they know their deadlines, there shouldn't be any problems. And I always tell them that if they think they've got problems to get in contact immediately so we can work out an alternative, and that reduces trouble too.'

Josh works with all kinds of marketing and other professionals, from advertising creatives to printers, from media analysts to on-site erectors who go around putting up signs at sporting events. 'My job is to delegate and manage from a distance,' he says. 'I have to make sure that everything is being considered and done at the right time within budget, from getting the print ordered to arranging to meet journalists so that, hopefully, we get some positive editorial coverage in the right magazines. I liaise between all the different departments and individuals and make sure that they are all doing what they should at the right time. I don't really have responsibility for making sure that what they do is right – my role is limited to making sure that things happen at the right time and the costings are within budget.'

Josh also works closely with the marketing managers to make sure that the project plan matches the strategic plan, which is the process of developing a strategic fit between the client's goals and the capabilities of the people and resources involved, and the changing market opportunities. 'Sometimes I suggest something which hasn't been thought of as part of the strategic plan, such as why don't we do some banner advertising on sporting sites which are going to be televised. Depending on the client, some exposure to sporting audiences can be very worthwhile. I can then arrange to have the banners printed and erected at sites all over the country. Sometimes there are local events going on that the marketing manager doesn't know about, like local festivals or fairs or sponsorship. I give feedback on marketing opportunities that I have come across to the marketing manager for approval and then execute them as part of the project or campaign.'

There are specific life cycle stages in each campaign which Josh recognises, from early enthusiasm to later realism, calling in contingency charges when the real costs exceed the estimates. 'Funnily enough, my favourite stage is the post-event analysis, when I write a report and analyse what we could have done better. There is always something, no matter how well it went, and often there are major improvements that could have been made. Then, next time, it is important to use the results of previous projects to make sure that subsequent ones work as well as possible.'

Josh has a regular salary but also gets a commission of a small percentage of everything that he manages to save from the budget the client has signed off. 'I am often able to make savings by ordering print from several clients' jobs from one printer in one run, with just a small few changes,' he says. 'I can also make sure that the media buyers purchase magazine and TV advertising slots which can be negotiated at a really good price, by putting several clients' adverts into one deal.'

He is also continually on the lookout for new suppliers. 'In order to keep the costs down it is good to have plenty of competition between the suppliers, like printers and other third parties. It keeps them on their toes and means that we can make extra savings.' However, Josh has to be careful that corners are not cut, sacrificing quality for price. 'It's my job to make sure that all the standards are maintained or even exceeded,' he says. 'If the marketing manager has any complaints from the client about some element of a job, they pass on the complaint to me and it's my role to sort it out.'

Josh says that a professional marketing background is best for a project manager, 'because I understand what the clients want and all the component parts that go into a campaign and how they work together'. But he has a junior assistant, Lisa, who has come straight from university after completing a degree in sociology. She expects to spend about 18 months with Josh before taking on a similar job elsewhere. Josh adds, 'My job might even be available, as I am thinking of moving to the country and becoming a lecturer in marketing and media studies at Exeter or Bristol University. If that happens then they'll need someone here, and who better than someone I've trained?' Lisa says, 'It would be brilliant if that happens because I really like the work. It is so structured and organised and I'm happy not having to be creative. I'm not the best original thinker, but I like backing up other people who are.' She is doing a part-time marketing course with the Open University which she is funding herself, although the firm gives her any time off that she needs. 'The courses are modular and recognised by the Chartered Institute of Marketing (CIM) and it helps make sense of what Josh is teaching me. I can see the campaigns from a helicopter perspective and see how the different elements fit together and understand about objectives and markets and so forth. It helps everything make more sense.'

Josh reports to the board and has to deliver regular reports on everyone that he works with as well as the campaigns that he has managed. 'I'm not very happy doing reports on people that I've worked with, but it is part of the job and the only way to make sure that there is continual improvement.'

Josh says that his job is incredibly varied and interesting. 'It is challenging sometimes and can be pressured, but never too much. I would keep doing it for many years more, but my wife wants to move to the country and I really do need to be in London to do this particular job.'

Skills you'll need

- Organisational and diplomatic skills are essential. Josh says, 'You can't get anyone to do what you want by bullying them. You have to be able to communicate accurately and clearly, both in writing and speech, and inspire people to give their best.'
- Josh learned his IT skills on the job. 'The company that supplied the project management software we use trained us to use it and then it was just a matter of practice.' Otherwise, Josh has to be able to use a word processor and e-mail.
- Josh doesn't speak any other languages and says that limits the projects he can work on. 'I would advise anyone coming into any branch of marketing to have at least one other

language. So many marketing campaigns are pan-European these days that more than one language is often essential.'

■ Everything in life is a project or can be expressed as such, and you can get good practice by turning everyday tasks and events into projects. How many people are involved in organising an outing to the cinema, for example, or a group of people going out to dinner? Imagine that other elements are involved, like advertising and promotion as well as the booking, getting people together, and then discussions afterwards.

Relationship marketing manager

Money: A junior with a degree might expect £14,000. With experience in general marketing you may start on £30,000. There are not many perks at a junior level but as you progress you could get a company car, health insurance and gym membership.

Hours: Officially likely to be 10–6 but there could be lots of overtime.

Health risk: Low. As with most office-based jobs, the biggest risk in driving to and from the office.

Pressure rating: Medium to high.

Glamour rating: Medium. Down at your local wine bar they're unlikely to have any idea what relationship marketing means.

Travel rating: Medium. You'll have to visit big clients, although most of your communications will be by e-mail and telephone. You may also go to international marketing shows and seminars to see the latest technology.

Relationship marketing is a new marketing concept which emerged in the 1990s, also known as **customer relationship marketing** *or* **CRM**. *It means that the focus is on the customer and creating customer pull rather than product push. It assumes that attracting a new customer is only the first stage and that the greatest effort must be in retaining existing customers. Statistics have shown that it is far cheaper to keep existing customers than it is to attract new ones, and it has become a marketing science in its own right.*

Selina Crawford started work as a marketing assistant for a computer software firm ten years ago and is now CRM manager. She says, 'Relationship management is all about moving the focus of the marketing from the single sale to customer retention. This means that instead of focusing on product or services features, we focus on the benefits and take a far longer view of the customers than we did before, hopefully making them lifetime customers instead of once-only purchasers.'

She explains that the use of CRM software has allowed relationship marketing to grow up. 'Now we can treat every single customer as a unique individual, and know an awful lot about every one, even if we have millions of customers.'

The emphasis for Selina is on customer service and

ensuring that the brand and company are the automatic preferred choice for as many people as possible.'Of course, we still promote the products and services and the company, but basically we try to create market pull from the customers rather than delivering market push.'

Previously, Selina had low levels of individual customer commitment and only moderate customer contact. These days her department has high levels of commitment and contact with each customer.'Previously, the quality of the product was only the concern of the product manager and the manufacturing team, but now product quality has become the concern of everyone on the marketing team.'

Technology is the key to relationship marketing, not just in terms of the CRM software but also in the use of the Internet to reach individual customers by e-mail and in integration with the back-office systems so that the CRM software has a full picture of a customer's activities. Selina says,'The CRM software needs to be linked to the warehouse, so that customers can be told accurately whether the goods they want are available, and to the accounting department so that orders are processed immediately and invoices raised (and hopefully paid) as fast as possible. That helps the cash flow of the whole business.'

Selina devises marketing campaigns which are individually targeted.'Sometimes they are financial incentives, sometimes bundles of goods and services which we know from their past buying patterns should appeal to that particular customer.'She works closely with the product and brand managers to make sure that the marketing campaigns and all the collateral copy, slogans and print that go with it match the product objectives and the needs of the particular target market.'Most of our products are sold to IT professionals,'she says,'but we also use different channels to market so we need to have different campaigns for resellers, distributors, partners and direct customers.

'The key word in relationship management is personalisation. I find it much more interesting than straight marketing, because I really feel that I am talking directly to specific individuals and in many cases that is exactly what I am doing.'While previously **market segmentation** divided target markets into, perhaps, eight or ten groups or categories according to income, age, or place of residence and through making demographic or lifestyle assumptions, these days relationship marketing is so precise that campaigns can be amended in many hundreds or thousands of ways to make them personal.

'Search engines on big databases linked to e-commerce transactions mean that most firms have all kinds of information available to them,' says Selina. 'From the moment a customer first registers at a site or makes a first purchase from a store, they are being analysed and measured.'

Selina's work as a relationship marketer has a lot in common with that of a customer service manager. She says, 'I have to anticipate what the customer might need and feed that back to product development. I try to differentiate the marketing campaign for every customer and make our marketing appear focused on each of them as individuals. In a way, it's all about flattering their egos and making them believe that they are unique, which of course they are.'

Once she knows that certain customers like certain products or shop at certain times of the day, for example, she can tailor the marketing so that it catches the eye of individuals. 'We can take it to the point where they almost feel psychologically linked to us and we find that they stay with us and purchase far more as loyal customers than before we adopted relationship marketing,' she says.

Selina explains that she loves her job for many reasons. 'It has great variety, I am working at the forefront of technology and I am using technology in innovative ways to attract and retain customers. I meet lots of people and spend my days on many different tasks. Some of them are creative, some operational, some technical, some very people oriented and some very solitary. Sometimes I work from home, when I am writing proposals and reports, other times I am out in meetings with our partners and resellers. I travel a fair bit and occasionally go to the USA to see the latest in relationship marketing. There is no doubt that America leads the field and I have to go to trade shows and seminars to see what they are doing and then bring it back here.'

Selina says that her job is to enhance the customer experience every time they interact with her firm. 'There is no doubt that the idea is to make as much money as we can from every customer, by cross-selling and introducing new products and services to them and it works.' She particularly likes the aspect of her work which focuses on intelligently analysing and assessing data to look for new sales opportunities. 'I don't just have to think up campaigns, which I was doing before. Now I have to spot links and patterns in the behaviour and see where new products could find a niche.'

Technology also means that it is possible automatically to record information about surfers who visit websites. **Cookies**, or small files stored on visitors' hard drives, contain a great deal of information, which is transferred to the sites they visit. They enable a website to recall information about users' activities across multiple visits. Selina says, 'A key aspect of relationship marketing that particularly interests me is permission-based marketing or offering opt-in services which require customers to specifically request offers and provide certain information to get the offers. This information can then be used in many ways to help product development and in developing other marketing campaigns.'

At a low level this means sending out personalised cards on customers' birthdays or, more interestingly, looking at how one purchase could indicate that a customer might be interested in a whole range of associated products. 'A customer who buys some software for a travel industry application might also be interested in paying for connection to other services for the travel industry,' Selina says. 'A lot of the work is in sideways cross-marketing.'

However, Selina is always aware that her customers, particularly electronic ones, are only three clicks away from her competitors. 'Everyone is working on relationship marketing these days, there is nothing special about it. We are still vulnerable to having our customers poached. We just have to work extra hard at keeping the ones we've got and seeing how we can win new ones from our competitors.'

Skills you'll need

- You'll probably be like Selina and already have general marketing training and qualifications before specialising in relationship marketing. But there are also opportunities for juniors and assistants with the right skills. These include inquisitiveness, tact and the ability to see the world from the customer's point of view. Selina says, 'There is a lot of time spent seeing how our customers view us and then making our marketing as appealing as possible to individuals.'

- Selina speaks three languages and says that she uses them a lot. 'Because I work for an international software house we have customers and partners all over the world and although English is the lingua franca, it always goes down well and appeals to them if I can at least try to speak to them in another language.' She spent her gap year between A levels and university in Japan and finds that experience comes in useful. 'In fact, I find that everything is useful,' she says. 'No experience is ever wasted.'

- Selina acquired a number of technology skills and also takes regular refresher courses with the Chartered Institute of Marketing (CIM). 'I believe in constant lifelong learning,' she says, 'and I believe that everybody, no matter how good they are or how much they know, can always learn something new.'

■ Relationship marketing requires people skills and intuition above all else, so do whatever you can to develop those. Investigate the technologies used for CRM and learn new ways of managing customers by reading the trade and technology press.

Glossary

■ **Cookie**
A small 'packet' of computer code, usually transmitted by e-mail, which instructs an IT system to do something. For example, every time customers log onto a certain website a cookie at the site might, unbeknown to them, take their e-mail details for future marketing use. The cookie might also automatically forward the customers' e-mail addresses to the marketing manager.

■ **Customer relationship management (CRM)**
The management of existing customers to ensure their loyalty.

■ **Market segmentation**
The process of subdividing a market into distinct subsets of customers who behave in similar ways, and have similar values, incomes or needs.

Research analyst

See *Market researcher*.

Research director

See *Market researcher*.

Sales director

Money: The big difference between a marketing and a sales role is the way the salary is structured. While a marketing person is usually on a flat salary, the salesperson is more likely to be on basic plus commission. The basic is likely to be from £5,000 to £10,000, and there may be other perks depending on the size and type of the company and the level of responsibility. A senior sales director might also get commission on the sales achievements of others in his team. Often salespeople earn more than marketing people, despite the low basic.

Hours: Varies, but often with overtime. Negotiate the amount of overtime you are expected to do before you accept the job and, if you think it is going to be too much, say so immediately.

Health risk: Low.

Pressure rating: Medium to high. Selling is hard work, hence the potentially good rewards.

Glamour rating: Medium. Sales used to have a poor image, but is increasingly being regarded with respect.

Travel rating: Varies from job to job. Usually medium to high although can be low. Some salespeople spend their whole time 'on the road' and only visit the head office rarely. Many 'operate' from home or a local office, using IT to communicate with the central computer. Others work permanently from a base office or shop, with the customers coming to them.

Sales and marketing are inextricably linked and often the two jobs are run together. All sales directors need to know about marketing and all marketing directors need to know what a sales director does, for if the sales function is not properly carried out, there is no income to pay the marketing director and his team.

Unusually, Briony Waters moved from marketing into sales – she says that she prefers to deal with people rather than concepts. But she still has to do a lot of marketing work in her job as a sales director. 'I have to work very closely with the marketing director, feed her some ideas which come out of my contact with the customers, and work to differentiate our firm, which sells cosmetics, from other similar firms.'

She works for an interior design partnership and says that she likes the emphasis on selling because it is all about relationships. 'As a salesperson I have to make relationships with potential customers, sustain relationships with existing customers and then nurture the relationships over time so that we develop mutual loyalty.' She says that marketing plays a crucial part in that. 'It is all about developing a brand and promoting it, so that the customers choose our image above that of our competitors.'

At university Briony studied psychology, which she says is essential for both sales and marketing. 'A salesperson has to know about a customer's wants and needs, about developing their awareness of a need in a subconscious way, about dovetailing the product or service personality with their need and how to use verbal and non-verbal communication to raise awareness of the need and realisation of our ability to resolve and satisfy it.'

Salespeople have to understand that marketing is the infrastructure through which sales are made. Sales are the result of good marketing and, although the salesperson is at the 'sharp end' of the business, sales and the salesperson's income depend hugely on good marketing. If there is one part of the job Briony dislikes it is trying to interest potential customers in something that has no appeal to them. 'I would never do cold calling,' she says. 'That's at the blunt end of sales and I'm not interested in that. But by combining marketing and psychology with sales, it can become a refined science.'

Briony adds that she likes the negotiating, which she compares with a game of chess. 'It's all about setting high parameters, discussing them, coming to a mutual agreement in which everyone feels they've got a good deal, closing the deal and then making sure that the customer is happy. I'm often dealing with a customer for a year or more, and all through that time the marketing is crucial.' She works with the marketing managers in many of the fabric and carpet supply firms and rebrands and passes on a lot of their products to her customers. 'I also have to go out and find new customers and that means a combination of our own branding and rebranding our suppliers' products.'

Sometimes she gets let down by her suppliers, and has to take responsibility. 'That's one part of the job I really don't like, when I promise something and then can't deliver through no fault of our own. But what I really do like is working with the rest of the marketing team to develop and enhance the campaigns that we are running, with the objective of converting new customers and selling in to existing clients too.'

Interior design embraces many different types of product, and Briony says that if a customer comes for a new kitchen, she can often end up selling a new bathroom, living room or bedroom. 'There is lots of switch-selling and cross-selling and extending sales over many years. The big thing I try to build is loyalty, and that can only be achieved when the customer trusts us to do a good job for the best price. We don't actually compete directly on price because we add a lot of service, but our image is of a firm which will be competitive but not compromise quality. We also try to be as honest as we can, so that if a customer has a dreadful idea we don't think will work, we tell them. So all the time I am reinforcing the marketing messages, helping develop new messages, looking for ideas where we can differentiate ourselves, and closing sales. Apart from the last part, it is no different from a marketing manager's job.'

IT plays an important part in Briony's job these days. She says, 'I go into a client's house with my laptop computer and can create a visual of what their new space will look like. I can show them colour samples and then check with the suppliers using a **WAP** link that the colour is available. The same goes for furniture. And then I can place the order then and there and give the customer a delivery date. I can raise an invoice in front of them and, of course, the sooner an invoice is raised the sooner we'll get paid.' She says that she learned to use the design and visualisation software 'on the job' but learned basic IT like word processing, time management and e-mail while at college. 'It's all basic stuff, really,' she adds.

About every week or so Briony has a meeting with her marketing and PR managers. 'We talk about new marketing initiatives and I tell them what is happening with the customers and we talk about new sales that the PR person can turn into press releases or editorial stories.'

In many firms the sales and marketing roles are combined, with the same person responsible for thinking up new campaigns and seeing them through to the sales. Briony believes that the advantage of this system is that the marketing can be judged more precisely in terms of sales figures. 'Although the sales and profits where I work are obviously a way of evaluating the success of the marketing, the two are still separated to some degree. That means that the marketing initiatives and campaigns can be focused on things like building brand and image, which are not immediately tangible in sales but have a big long-term impact. I prefer to work with firms that take that long-term view.'

Briony remembers her time as a junior in a marketing department. 'I really was the junior and had to run around making tea and coffee, collecting the post, doing all the most boring and mundane jobs. But all the time I was being judged and evaluated and they offered me the formal marketing training in time. I found the study easy, it's all common sense really.' Now Briony has several certificates in various aspects of marketing, but says that it is the front line of selling that interests her most. 'It is very exciting and such a buzz when I make a big sale and, of course, the commission makes it very interesting.' She denies that she makes a shed-load on every deal, but she drives a brand-new Audi in preference to the Ford which she was offered as a company car. 'I also have plenty of holidays and I'm about to move into a new flat. Selling is a good life,' she adds.

Skills you'll need

- While the ability to develop relationships and negotiate deals so that everyone feels they are in a win-win situation is obviously important, Briony says that probably the most important skill is the ability to listen. 'Failure to listen is arguably one of the greatest causes of misunderstanding and problems later down the sales cycle.'
- The ability to concentrate and think on your feet, putting together complex deals and expressing them in simple terms in such a way that they are irresistible.
- The ability to interpret non-verbal signals and to communicate clearly verbally, and electronically too. Basic IT skills at a user level are essential, but you won't have to do any programming.
- You'll need to look and sound confident, be assertive and be able to build a rapport with people. A confident image is helpful in several ways: people will trust you and believe that you are competent.
- Because this is a 'front line' job, requiring constant contact with clients, dress code is crucial, varying according to the company you work for and the products they sell. Some firms require strictly formal dress, with nothing less than a suit. Other enterprises, however, are more relaxed and smart casual will do. Briony says that she wears very smart casual clothing. 'I don't actually wear a suit, but the next best thing. The point is to look very neat, tidy and clean. Anything less is unacceptable.'
- It is possible to learn to be assertive, but you must have a fundamental core of toughness. You will need to have a thick skin to accept rejections without taking them personally. You have to be aggressive enough to get your point across without making an unpleasant impression and loud enough to have people take notice of you without being off-putting.
- You have to be determined and resilient, able to take knocks and setbacks and still bounce back.

Tips

- Practise, practise, practise selling anything. If you are looking for holiday or gap year work, try to get sales jobs. It is all about experience and confidence and the more you can get the better.

- In life generally, think about positive not negative outcomes.
- Do whatever you can to develop your powers of persuasion. The best way to do this is by selling things and convincing people that they really wanted whatever you sold them and are happy with the price.

Glossary

- **WAP technology**

  Wireless application protocol, likely to be the biggest leap in communications since the advent of the mobile phone. It allows individuals to log onto the Internet from any location, using their mobile or desktop PC, accessing data that may be personally tailored.

Sales promotional director

Money: If you join a sales promotion department or agency as a junior, you'll probably start on £14,000 and be expected to be a dogsbody. But with marketing experience, even a first job in sales promotion could get you £18,000, quickly rising to £22,000–£25,000. People pay for ideas, so if you can keep coming up with fresh and novel schemes, you can demand a good income. The ability to execute them is also important, but there are always others around who can help with that – it is the ability to have original and effective concepts which commands the high salaries. Ultimately, you could reach board level on £45,000–£55,000. Perks vary according to experience and client – even as a junior you might get computer games, for example, if your client is a software company. At a more senior level you'd get health insurance, a company car and gym membership as well.

Hours: Regular 10–6 at the beginning, but quickly requiring more overtime as you become more senior.

Health risk: Low.

Pressure rating: Medium reaching high as several campaigns start running at the same time, new clients need proposals and staff have to be managed.

Glamour rating: Depending on the client, medium to high. Sales promotion is often the most high-profile of all marketing activities.

Travel rating: Varies considerably according to the job, agency, client and stages of a campaign. You might be entirely office based, with all meetings limited to internal ones, or you might be 'on the road' a lot of the time, going round to stores and retail outlets delivering sales promotion materials.

Sales promotion is a science occupying the space between marketing and sales. It aims to motivate the sales force and make their efforts more effective and entice the customers with special offers and other short-term deals.

Sales promotion is a complex and delicate art, a specialist arm of marketing which is a career in itself. Helen Fowler works for a specialist sales promotion agency, but spent four years in a large marketing agency in an internal department focused on sales promotion activity. She says, 'Modern marketing is about more than just having a good product at a good price which looks good and is easily available to customers. The product also has to be promoted so that it has some special unique selling point which sets it apart from competitors in the same market space.'

Helen's job involves thinking up new promotional campaigns which will help the sales force to approach new customers or return to existing ones, and seeing those campaigns through. She says, 'There is a promotional mix which is a blend of advertising, personal selling, promotion and PR and within each there are specific tools such as point-of-sale materials, coupons, competitions, demonstrations, flashes and so on. It's my job to know all about them and how best to use them.'

Helen did a degree in marketing with psychology, which she says she thoroughly enjoyed and which is very useful now that she's at work. 'We studied all kinds of things, from the formal theory of marketing to how to encode messages in the marketing devices so that customers are not even aware that they are being sold to.'

Helen works closely with the marketing, product and brand managers in agencies, and directly with clients. 'There are a lot of meetings, at which I am expected to make presentations. I have to develop proposals, including budgets, work out a plan for the execution of a promotion and then afterwards wrap it up with a report. I often have to present that too if we are to get more business from that agency or client.' However, at the beginning, when she was just an assistant in a large agency, her work had far less responsibility. 'At the beginning I worked regular hours, did what I was told and was occasionally invited to give my point of view. Gradually I was given more which I gladly took on and was very serious about doing a good job.'

Helen believes that the ability to mix with all types of people and have a good laugh with most of them helps her a lot. 'It's all about relationships at the end of the day and although I have to come up with some original ideas it is just as important that they are executed properly and that means working with people. And if you can have a good time while you are doing the work, that makes sense, doesn't it?'

Helen has always gone out for drinks with her colleagues after work. 'Actually, I don't drink alcohol any more but I just enjoy the culture and the fun after work.' Her boyfriend works for the same sales promotion agency, and they live, work and socialise together. 'It wouldn't work for everyone but it works for us,' she says.

Sales promotion is a challenge, emphasises Helen, and it is also rewarding because the results can be evaluated directly in the sales figures. 'We work for a lot of different companies selling a lot of different products, and every campaign has something new about it, although of course there is a limit to the number of special offers and competitions we can think of.'

Helen also works on teaser campaigns, creating a puzzle in the advertising or point-of-sale material that the customer wants to solve. 'Teasers can be risky because they can antagonise people, but if you get a good one then people can remember it for years.' Her objective is to make the teaser complement the brand image and objectives and appeal directly to the target market. 'Not always easy,' she says.

For Helen, sales promotion is a fun job and she likes the variety of the environment. 'You've got to be outgoing and positive, and be able to come up with some innovative ideas,' she says. 'If you can do that then a career in sales promotion can be well paid and hugely enjoyable. I love it.'

Skills you'll need

- An outgoing 'bubbly' temperament is helpful though not essential. You've got to like meeting people, though, and find it easy to get along with all sorts. Some of your meetings will be very formal, with new clients, others with the third parties who manage the campaigns or the printers who create the collateral material for them. Then there will be the office politics to contend with – being a sales promotion manager means having eyes in the back of your head and a brain like a computer.
- Language and IT skills are highly desirable. Many agencies and clients are pan-European these days and you'll need the language skills to help in meetings and to make sure that the local language collateral material is accurate. Basic IT word processing and e-mail skills are essential and the ability to use a spreadsheet and project management and time manager software would be a bonus.
- You have to be able to sell ideas and then see them through, so powers of persuasion are necessary to back up the creative juices. You have to be able to network, to find more business, and to have a good head for money and figures.
- Grasp of formal marketing theory is helpful before specialisation in sales promotion. You have to understand classics like product life cycle, **market segmentation**, push and pull strategies and so forth, and how to communicate in many formats.
- The ability to read research and write proposals and reports is essential, but can be learned on the job as a junior. The power to make effective presentations counts for a lot.

■ Start looking out for sales promotions and ask yourself what is involved and how effective they are. Keep a notebook on sales promotions – you will be surprised by how useful it will be in years to come, for many of today's promotions are simply recycled ideas from ten or 15 years ago. What goes around comes around, so start making notes on all the promotions you see on television, in shops and stores and which come through the post or over the Internet.

Glossary

■ **Market segmentation**
The process of subdividing a market into distinct subsets of customers who behave in similar ways, and have similar values, incomes or needs.

Sampler / tester

Money:	Often an hourly rate, which reflects the low status of the job, ranging from £5 to £10 an hour, depending on the area of the country and the initiative and responsibility involved.
Hours:	Vary enormously, but often part-time or casual.
Health risk:	Low.
Pressure rating:	Low.
Glamour rating:	Low.
Travel rating:	Low to medium. Some testers have to travel extensively through the UK to produce a pan-UK report on how products are received in different parts of the country, but usually travel is limited to the area where the tester is located.

It is all too easy for marketing professionals to sit in their ivory towers pontificating about trends, fashions, yields and budgets. To be really in touch they have to get out in the field and pose as consumers.

We are all consumers, of course, but it is surprising how many marketing campaigns simply pass us by because we are not in the target market group. For every campaign that you are aware of, there are probably 40 or 50 more of which you're not. So every marketing department or agency needs a group of samplers or testers who are part of the target group and can give feedback on the consumer experience.

Alex von Duren worked as a tester while he was at Leeds University doing a marketing degree, which not only prevented him getting into debt while he studied, but was also valuable experience for his course. He says, 'I worked for a large agency based in Leeds, where I was studying. They used me about five or six times a month, for a whole day at a time, and I did more work for them in the holidays managing focus groups.'

Alex got the job as a sampler by contacting the agency when he first got to Leeds. 'It was either that or a job in a bar and this was much more fun and helped my degree work.'

His tasks varied. 'Sometimes I had to actually go into stores and report on how the point-of-sale merchandising looked. Other times I had to do blind sampling of a selection of similar products and say which I thought was best and why. It was all very scientific, with complicated report forms which had to be completed.'

All the products that Alex tested were aimed at the teens and twenties market and ranged from men's cosmetics and shampoo to convenience foods and power tools. 'Some were not products I would normally have used for myself, so one has to put one's own preference to one side a bit, but there is always some element of personal preference involved.' The agency always used other testers and samplers too, so that the result was an average or median view.

'When I was running focus groups it was the same sort of work,' says Alex. 'I had to work with a group of people and ask their views of the products and the messages and slogans that the agency was planning to use. It is very easy for the marketing managers to think up sales messages and slogans which sound awful in the real world.'

When Alex graduated with a first, he joined the agency immediately as a marketing executive, became a marketing manager, then a group marketing manager responsible for other executives and several accounts. He says, 'My early experience as a sampler was not only fun, it helped put my course into perspective. I was able to talk to marketing professionals who were actually out there doing the job and that was great. It gave the course more point while I was doing it.'

Skills you'll need

- Confidence is the main thing. You have to cope with situations which involve your initiating contact with strangers and asking their views on products.
- When it comes to giving your own views, you'll have to have the strength of character and personality to make dispassionate judgments without being influenced by others.
- Good verbal and written communications skills will be essential, plus the ability to remain independent while still giving a view. Tact, discretion and charm are all useful attributes too.

Tips

- Start noticing marketing campaigns and come to a view as to whether each one is an effective advertisement or promotion. Compile reports, either mentally or on paper or computer, on what your opinions are. Practise the art of reviewing and summarising and making suggestions for improvements.
- Many agencies are looking for samplers and testers of all ages, so start your marketing career as soon as you like by approaching local agencies and asking whether they need casual or part-time staff.

Spin doctor

Money: This is usually a fairly high-flying PR job arrived at after several years working your way up. So you could expect to start on around £40,000 and, depending on your experience and track record, achieve £80,000+ if you decide to start your own business.

Hours: Endless. There is no such thing as office and personal hours in this type of job. You'll have to be there for the client when they need you, and that may mean press conferences at any time of the day.

Health risk: Medium. The enemy is stress, so your vulnerability depends on how you handle pressure.

Pressure rating: Medium to high. You could find yourself the buffer between a client in trouble and a press pack baying for blood. It will be up to you to do the right thing to improve the situation.

Glamour rating: Depends. To some, the spin doctors are the opposite of glamorous – they are the lowest of the low. To others, this is the pinnacle of PR and marketing.

Travel rating: Medium. It depends on who your clients are.

This is not likely to be a job that you see advertised, but many marketing and PR firms specialise in message development work or helping to massage a message so that the target market gets exactly the image or impression that is wanted. Often the spin doctors are called in when a client is in trouble, but they would say that their skills are needed from the first stage in every campaign.

All marketing professionals have a touch of the spin doctor about them. It is a subtle skill which is actually at the heart of marketing – persuading people that this product or that service is the best there is and essential for their wellbeing. Unfortunately, spinning has developed a bad reputation for distorting the truth and spin doctors are often the last resort of a beleaguered product or service which is in crisis. Ted Bailey works for a large PR agency which specialises in crisis management, but he is about to move to a marketing agency where he is going to use his 'spinning' skills in a strategic planning role. He says, 'I hate being called a spin doctor because it demeans what I do, which is a very valuable service to companies which are in trouble. Sometimes it is a product which is having to be recalled because of a fault or it is a firm which is having to make a number of employees redundant. The point is that the company wants to come out of the experience without any slur on their reputation or, if possible, with their reputation even enhanced.'

Ted became a spin doctor by being an especially good PR person. 'I just developed a talent for seeing the positive in any situation or coming up with slogans and messages which turn a flaky situation into something strong and good. The trick is, though, to do that without looking cheap or as if you are just trying to get something good out of a bad situation.' Sometimes it is best to be honest and frank, to clear the way for a new positive image to emerge. 'People think that spin doctors are just liars who will say anything to get their client off the hook, but that's not so. We just try to emphasise the positive and don't focus on the negative.'

To do his job well, Ted needs particularly good relationships with the press. 'The media is crucial in getting a good message across and they have to trust me. Sometimes I have to take decisions which will protect my reputation rather than that of my client, but that's the way it is.' He gives as an example a local councillor who was accused of theft and malpractice. 'He was found innocent, or rather the police decided not to press charges, but he was concerned that his reputation had been permanently damaged and he hired me to improve his image. I had him doing some good works, lots of photo opportunities with children, and got him some media interviews as someone who supported the equal rights of women in local councils. That was five years ago and now no one remembers the problems he once had. He has a squeaky-clean image and is highly respected by the community.'

In his new job Ted is going to be working on strategic campaign development. He says, 'I will be taking the original brief from the clients on what their objectives are and then will sit down and work out what the campaign should consist of. There may be some slogan development work, then a whole lot of television advertising, for example. I would also work with the advertising professionals to get a campaign that matched the client's profile and met their aims. I'd also work with the sales promotional people, devising sales development campaigns. I wouldn't be responsible for making sure it all happened – I'd pass things on to the campaign manager who would make sure that things happen in the right order and at the right time.'

IT is important to Ted, particularly for the speed and efficiency of communication that it offers. 'I have had to learn about IT as I went along and I wish I had had some formal training in what works best. I'd like to know more about IT marketing.'

Ted's time is currently split fairly equally between meetings with clients and other marketing professionals, and researching and writing quietly at his desk. 'I often work at home,' he says. In the office, he is rarely able to find a quiet place to sit and think or write strategy plans. 'I do my best thinking late at night in front of the television, so I count that as part of my working day.'

Ted says he likes the variety of his job and the need to think laterally. 'I often have to come at a problem from a completely different perspective, but I am looking forward to working out solutions without starting from a drama.'

Skills you'll need

- An outgoing, confident, positive personality is needed to handle the challenge of being a spin doctor. Ted says, 'I find I often have to show energy and enthusiasm when I feel them least and inside I know that things are looking a lot bleaker than I'm painting them. But that's my job.'
- The ability to think before speaking and filter out anything that would not help the situation is helpful. You have to be able to focus on the impact of what you are planning, saying or doing on others, particularly the target market of your client. You have to try to establish a positive rapport with them through the messages you use.
- You'll need to have first-class communications skills, to the level where they are innate and not learned. You'll have to enjoy talking to the press and thinking on your feet, and be able to calm and reassure clients who are in a personal and professional crisis. You have to make yourself clearly understood and be able to understand others, and this comes from a knowledge of people and how they react to situations and circumstances.

Tips

- When disasters happen (and there is something in the papers every day which could be considered a disaster by individuals, companies or products) think how you would handle the situation. Work out your strategy for dealing with it, and devise a plan of action.
- Develop your lateral thinking skills with exercises and courses.

Sponsorship manager

Money: As you probably already have a couple of years' experience in broad-based marketing, you'll probably start at £18,000–£20,000, rising to £35,000 or a little more. There are plenty of perks as part of the corporate hospitality.

Hours: Flexible. There will be plenty of office work with standard 9–5 hours, plus overtime when the sponsored events are taking place – often evenings or weekends. You'll also have to meet up with key journalists and entertain the sponsoring client.

Health risk: Low, unless the sponsored event features a high-risk sport and you get too near.

Pressure rating: Medium, but with plenty of opportunity to relax when the event takes place.

Glamour rating: High. There is no point in sponsorship unless it attracts lots of publicity, so you can be sure of contact with famous people and outings to famous places. Imagine the Mercury Music Awards, for example – lots of famous bands, slots on TV and radio and press liaison work. But first that deal had to be arranged, the price agreed and the obligations on both sides defined.

Travel rating: High. You will have to do your apprenticeship in the office and even when you are established there will always be a proportion of the work which is mundane and routine, but there will also be plenty of chances to get out and travel on expenses to glamorous places with glamorous people.

You've seen them – hot-air balloons, racing cars or tennis players with logos strategically placed all over them. The art of negotiating the best sponsorship deals is a specialist marketing art and a job in itself.

Kevin Best is managing director of a specialist sponsorship agency. He says, 'It is possible to start straight into a career in sponsorship but you'd have to begin at the bottom as a dogsbody trainee. Most sponsorship marketers have a background in general marketing before they specialise.

'Whichever way in you choose – straight from college or university as a trainee or after a couple of years in general marketing or PR – the sponsorship sector is high profile and involves big money.' It's true that it can cost millions to sponsor a major sporting event, but there are plenty of more modest opportunities to raise the profile of a brand in the public's consciousness and in a positive way.

Sponsorship is always fraught with problems, however. Imagine being the sponsor of an event where there was a serious accident and people were killed. The company name and brand would forever be linked with disaster and tragedy. Or you may invest thousands in a racing car or football team which was consistently last and be locked into a ten-year deal. So the sponsorship manager has to be able to take a pragmatic view on whether the opportunity is going to be beneficial in the long run, as well as being a good deal financially. Best says, 'It is a stressful job, but it can also be glamorous and you can find yourself on the inside of some really interesting events and occasions.' For sponsorship is not limited to sporting events. The arts, such as opera and pop, literary festivals and individuals who are undertaking some notable challenge, are often looking for sponsorship money.

In return for donating money the sponsor might get the event's name changed to their brand (the Martel Grand National, the Hennessy Gold Cup) or they might just get brand logos plastered all over the place (remember the John Player Special racing cars?). The logo may also appear on all marketing material and in other promotional and publicity material. The objective is to get as much brand exposure as you can for the bucks you are investing.

The sponsorship manager has the experience to know what makes a good investment deal, and the statistics on exposure to potential customers and how many are likely to convert to being loyal buyers. Best says, 'You have to have the best negotiating skills, because the sponsoring company wants as much from the deal as possible, with the minimum financial input. The sponsorship manager will have to develop a contract that everyone agrees to and is pleased with. The aim is a win-win situation.'

Quantifying the return on investment can be tricky. 'There is no real objective measure,' says Best. 'But there can be lots of anecdotal feedback. We do research on brand awareness before and after the sponsorship and that gives some measure.'

Some firms like to sponsor local people and events, others go for events which have some connection with the sector that their products are in, or the target market. Some large enterprises have an in-house person dedicated to managing their sponsorship deals, while others go through agencies which act as marriage brokers.

The sponsorship manager has to work closely with the account, brand and product managers. They will be representing the brand in negotiations with the individual or organisation looking for the cash. The person seeking the funding will have to demonstrate that the audience is suitable for the brand, that the brand will be enhanced and that there is going to be value in the deal.

Once the deal is organised and contracts signed, there will still be plenty of work to do in managing the agreement. Sponsoring a cricket tournament, for example, involves a whole summer of matches, press calls and publicity. The deal is only the first stage. Many sponsorship deals go on for many years or are repeated year after year, like the Robinson barley water deal with Wimbledon, which lasted more than 20 years. The job requires standard marketing and publicity skills, so that the best mileage can be achieved from the investment. Best says, 'You'll have to deal with journalists as well as clients and the people being sponsored, whose marketing talents might be almost non-existent.'

In the future, sponsorship is likely to play a big part in the expansion of digital television, providing important funds for entire channels as well as individual films and programmes. It might also be responsible for the survival of some high-cost sports, like motor racing, which could not survive without sponsorship.

Best says, 'Sponsorship can be a big black hole for money, because once a commitment is made it can be difficult to pull out without damaging the brand.' But for the marketing person arranging and managing the deals, it can be a lot of fun. There is invariably a great deal of 'corporate hospitality' going on alongside the sponsored event, and whether it is tennis, yachting, rowing, football, opera or Arctic exploration, there are bound to be opportunities for high-profile customers and the press to be invited. Best says, 'It may be strawberries and cream and champagne or it may be a special corporate box at the Albert Hall, but sponsorship always means gloss and glamour, otherwise there would be no point in doing it.'

Skills you'll need

- You'll have to be able to negotiate a good deal that leaves everyone smiling. You'll need excellent people skills, with plenty of natural charm. Underneath all that, though, you must be perceptive, have an analytical mind and a good eye for detail.
- You'll have to be a master of the PC and e-mail, although you won't require technical or programming skills. You'll need to know what IT can do.

- You'll have to be able to analyse statistics, read research and make sense of it and use your judgment to determine what is worth sponsoring to the best and most appropriate benefit of the brand.

- Anything that is going to improve your negotiating skills will stand you in good stead. Best recommends media sales training: 'There is nothing better than the training for selling advertising space to get the best negotiating skills for sponsorship deals. They know just how far to push to get a win-win deal for everyone.'

Stealth marketer

Money: £10,000 as a junior, rising to around £45,000 after eight years or so.

Hours: Probably regular 9–5 office hours, but whether at work or play you'll constantly be looking for opportunities for unusual marketing strategies.

Health risk: Other than the dangers of eating and drinking too much, this is a healthy job.

Pressure rating: Medium. Provided the ideas are coming through there is little stress apart from deadlines.

Glamour rating: Medium. Effectively you're a back-room person, but if you come up with a particularly effective campaign you may hit the trade papers.

Travel rating: Medium. You'll get to trade shows, probably, but many stealth marketers travel very little and spend all their time in offices.

As consumers become more sophisticated, marketers have continually to look for more subtle ways to get their messages across.

After university, Gabrielle White became a conventional marketing assistant and then a marketing manager in a medium-sized agency, where she tried her hand at most jobs. 'I would always recommend a medium agency of about 80 to 100 employees. It is large enough to have some decent clients and good managers, but small enough to get around to all the departments and try all the specialisations.'

While Gabbie's job title is still just marketing manager, her work now involves looking out for and putting into action all kinds of devious strategies which achieve publicity and editorial without the readers or viewers being aware of it. 'Sometimes, even the editors are not aware of what we are doing,' she says.

Product placement is an example of early stealth marketing, says Gabbie, and sponsorship is another. 'The idea is to get products in films or on TV sets, being used by the actors. Or, in a sponsorship situation, the logo being seen on motor racing cars or on sports heroes' clothing. There is an almost subliminal promotional effect, although people are often aware of what they are seeing. There is a very positive reinforcement of the sales and marketing message if film stars, soap actors and sporting heroes are seen to be using certain products.'

But consumers are getting used to product placement and sponsorship, so marketers have had to think even more subtly. Gabbie says, 'I spend a lot of time looking through magazines and newspapers and watching TV and radio, to look for opportunities for the managers in our client companies to have their say.' She uses professional freelance journalists to ghost-write opinion pieces and letters for publication on behalf of her clients. The reward is a one-line credit at the end of a published letter or a small byline on an opinion or viewpoint in a magazine. But, says Gabbie, stealth marketing is now reaching the point where even the company name or product brand are not mentioned. 'There was an example during the last Olympics, which was not arranged by us but is the sort of thing we do. BBC Television ran a five-minute film which highlighted certain leading sportspeople. Actually, all the sportspeople in the film were sponsored by a sportswear company, but the name was never mentioned and the logo, which is instantly recognisable, was never shown, and yet the client was extremely pleased. The film was shown on BBC TV, after all, and showed only the people sponsored by the sportswear company. That's pretty good stealth marketing, if you ask me.'

As well as monitoring magazines, newspapers and other media for opportunities, Gabbie spends a lot of time in brainstorming meetings and working with other marketers and their clients on new strategies. 'I don't actually have any clients of my own any more. I am a sort of floating marketer, helping all the other marketing managers with their clients. I'm an ideas person now. In fact I rarely have to see a strategy through to completion. I leave that to the campaign or project manager or the account marketing manager.'

Gabbie works closely with a small group of editors and TV and radio researchers, who she knows are always on the lookout for good new ideas. 'They all want to be different, they have very small budgets and they need ideas to make them stand apart from their competition. I have talented, often opinionated and personable people with big budgets to spend and I have to think of the ideas which allow them to work symbiotically together.' Consequently, Gabbie's job involves plenty of wining and dining, as well as attending long-winded marketing meetings and strategy planning meetings. 'I rarely find that I get my ideas actually in a meeting. All they are good for is selling the idea to those who sanction and run them. My job is to think of new schemes which will give a client publicity in a subtle way. The thing is, it can be so subtle that most consumers can miss it, but that doesn't really matter.'

Gabbie is planning to start a specialist marketing company with a couple of friends. 'We are going to specialise in stealth and guerrilla marketing,' she says. 'It is the future of marketing, thinking up newer, more bizarre ideas and plans for spreading the name of a client in a positive way to the widest audience.'

Skills you'll need

- It is essential to have the ability to think laterally and come up with new ideas. You also need the ability to work with plenty of different types of client and inspire them to see the potential in your ideas. Yet you must also be able to see that a particular idea does not 'have legs' and won't work, and start thinking of others instead.
- You need to be a business person first and a nuts-and-bolts marketer second. Gabbie says, 'I have to think like a consumer and then think like the client and see where the interests of the first can be served by the interests of the second. It's easy really, but it helps if you have a completely free hand, like I have.'
- Gabbie studied classical languages and arts at university, which she says gave her a broad education with good self-discipline and attention to detail.
- You need self-confidence and the ability to ask obvious questions and to question everything that is accepted. 'You must not be afraid to ask questions. I treat every meeting as an opportunity to learn,' Gabbie says.
- Gabbie is very interested in new technologies and works hard to incorporate the Internet and **WAP** into her projects. 'Some campaigns are limited to traditional media, but most clients want to see new technology being used, either in a small way or with the whole campaign almost entirely based on it. So I have to know all about the power of the technology, if not the details of how it works.'

Tips

- As you move around your agency or department, make friends with those who matter. Networking isn't just a technical discipline. You need to know who the decision-makers are in the organisation and who will help you get what you want in your career.
- Use every industry event, new project and meeting as a learning experience and a chance to meet new people. Once you've established who the relevant experts are, cultivate the relationships and show interest in the individuals. You never

know when these contacts will prove useful. So never fall into the trap of bad-mouthing or criticising a job or individual on your way up or you will be out before you know it. You never know when you might want to make contact with people again.

Glossary

- **WAP technology**
  Wireless application protocol, likely to be the biggest leap in communications since the advent of the mobile phone. It allows individuals to log onto the Internet from any location, using their mobile or desktop PC, accessing data that may be personally tailored.

Telemarketer

Money: Often part-time and linked to the amount of time spent on the phone or the number of calls made. Starts at around £10,000. A good caller closing sales can reach £35,000. Someone doing less calling and more strategic planning and managing would earn £28,000.

Hours: Mainly regular 9–5 office hours, but many telemarketers have to work evenings and weekends. Shiftwork is common.

Health risk: Sitting at a desk for too long has an unwanted effect on your body shape, but that can be countered by regular work-outs at the gym.

Pressure rating: Medium. The stress of cold calling is hard to measure and varies from person to person, but combined with the low job satisfaction it can make this a difficult job.

Glamour rating: Low. Even if you are calling about the most glamorous products, few regard telemarketing as a sought-after job.

Travel rating: Low. Probably zero, actually. The whole point of telemarketing is that it is done on the telephone and the marketers don't have to travel, although if you're a manager you may have to go to client meetings to discuss new campaigns and strategies.

In simple terms, this means telephone selling. It's not glamorous and there can't be many people who see this as the pinnacle of their marketing career, but it can be a useful transitional job and a way of understanding human reactions to marketing messages and campaigns.

At its worst, this is the twenty-first-century version of the sweat shop, with hundreds of people chained to their desks by the telephone, doing repetitive, unsatisfying work, often trying to cold sell direct to potential customers. That's what happens in a lot of the call centres where telemarketers often work. Their calls are logged and managers listen in to make sure that they are saying the right thing. The job requires the hide of a rhinoceros. But that's telemarketing at its worst. There are also jobs in telemarketing where you are calling up people who have already indicated that they are interested, so you are not cold calling, and some may be involved in devising the campaigns, which is more interesting.

For the latter you need a thorough understanding of psychology, because you'll be devising the scripts that the telemarketers will be using. You'll know the responses that customers are likely to give and the appropriate answers from

How to get into Marketing and PR

the telemarketers to make sure that customers don't hang up and that they go on and buy something.

Petra Hollingsworth works as a telemarketing manager for a large agency which undertakes telemarketing projects for marketing and PR agencies and, for the length of the contracts at least, becomes the telemarketing arm of that company or their clients. As far as the customers on the end of the telephone are concerned, the calls are coming straight from the client firm. Petra says, 'It's true that we have a lot of clients who are trying to sell double glazing or garden furniture, new kitchens or sofas, but we also have others who use telemarketing to follow up on sales leads and to do some market research to gauge the feeling of consumers.'

Petra is responsible for a group of 15 telecallers and she says that it can be good fun in the office, even though the main work is often dull. 'We get a lot of students and out-of-work actors and they can liven the place up,' she says. She started on the telephones and then progressed. 'I did psychology at university and started working here in my final year to get some money. Then I started full-time because the money was quite good, and did a marketing course in my spare time by distance learning.'

Now Petra works with the clients to determine objectives, devise the scripts and monitor the telemarketers on the phones. 'You have to be quite tough because people are often rude, but then others are really nice and that makes up for it,' she says.

Some people say that telemarketing, at least at the front end, lacks responsibility and is unsatisfying, but Petra disagrees. 'Most of the work we do here is to close deals and follow up on people who have filled in forms for promotions,' she says. 'They are often interested in the product and want a chat.

'The job has a bad reputation but it's not justified. It can be a rewarding side of marketing, particularly when you are closing sales.'

Skills you'll need

- Petra says that this job is not for those without a thick skin and a robust temperament to take the knocks. 'You also need an understanding of the law, to know how you can legally use the data you receive.'
- A lateral mind, to work out new strategies and ways to interest people, is invaluable and an interest in psychology is always useful, so that you'll know how best to respond to objections to calls.

■ Some people just love the telephone, but there are accepted techniques and scripts and some voices are better than others for reassuring and persuading. Investigate which these are and practise making your voice appealing and calming.

Viral marketer

Money: After ten years as a marketing executive you might expect to earn £55,000. Viral marketing is unlikely to be a first job. You have to understand all the formal aspects of classical marketing before you can start. At this point you can expect plenty of perks, probably including a company car, six weeks' holiday, health insurance and gym membership.

Hours: Fairly conventional, which might mean a basic 10–6, but you should expect to be willing to work whenever the inspiration takes you or whenever pressure and deadlines demand it.

Health risk: Low.

Pressure rating: Medium to high. You'll be responsible for conception, implementation and return on investment of viral campaigns and sometimes they do not go smoothly.

Glamour rating: Medium. Some people assume that there is something unpleasant about viral marketing; others see it as being exciting and at the cutting edge of marketing innovation.

Travel rating: Low to medium. Other than taking clients to lunch and sometimes attending trade shows and seminars, you'll travel very little.

Word-of-mouth was the first form of viral marketing – the idea being that some marketing ideas and messages spread themselves like viruses around communities and markets. These days it is becoming a science in its own right.

Milo Hammond says that today's viral marketing strategies are often built on lists which are put together for other purposes and require e-mail and the Internet to spread them. 'People talk about computers having viruses as though they are the worst thing possible, but for a marketing professional a computer virus with a marketing message is a very successful thing.'

Milo says that although viruses are generally unloved they are a critical part of the marketing process and can bring spectacular results without much effort or outlay. 'Well used, the technique is powerful, but used badly it's like a plague,' he says. Some marketing professionals claim that the term viral marketing is just a fancy new way of describing word-of-mouth, but Milo points out that there are many aspects to it which make it successful. 'Viral marketing at its best grows like a wild weed, although the seeds have to be planted first and that's what I do.'An old-fashioned whisper campaign was the first way that a word-of-mouth viral marketing effort was started – and not much has changed.

The speed and penetration of viral marketing campaigns is unpredictable and hard to measure. Sometimes they start slowly and then escalate and become fashionable; other times they appear to take off fast but then splutter and falter, dying on their legs. Viral marketing also entails using your customers to sell for you by recommending you to their friends and spreading the word without asking. This can be triggered by good customer support or customer relationship management, but the viral message can just as easily be negative if the customer has had a bad experience.

Milo says, 'E-mails get sent around the world and many individuals and companies have mailing lists which mean that one message can get bounced on and on. The messages have to be specially written, however, so that they do not cause offence.' Milo's background is Oxbridge, where he studied classics before starting on a fast-track programme in a leading international marketing consultancy. He worked on viral marketing for his thesis. 'I looked at how viral marketing is an old concept and has been used through the centuries in different ways, for political purposes mainly, as well as how it can be adapted for modern commerce and capitalism,' he says. 'Viral marketing is a cool way of getting your product or service to market itself by exploiting the connections between like-minded people.'

Milo dislikes the term viral marketer as a job title. 'It's easy to call it "virile marketer", which of course I am but don't want as a job title,' he jokes. 'I prefer just being called a marketing executive, specialising in viral marketing.' In the agency that he works for, Milo deals with all the clients, advising on how their strategies can be extended and adapted to include a viral element. 'A good understanding of the law and technology are vital,' he says in conclusion.

Skills you'll need

- You need excellent communications skills and a good general education. This is a sophisticated job requiring an urbane and cultured approach if it is not to appear crass and offensive.
- Milo says that his degree taught him the necessary writing, analysis and communications skills. Since leaving Oxbridge he has taken a masters in marketing with a strong technology aspect, which has taught him everything he needs to know about how technology can be used to perpetuate and disseminate.

How to get into Marketing and PR

- 'It's not all technology, though,' says Milo. 'I also like to have advertising campaigns that get people asking questions and television campaigns that make people respond.'

Tips

- Milo says, 'I always practise by spreading so-called gossip and seeing how long it takes for some messages to get back to me – some never do – or return inaccurately. There are certain things that people want to repeat and things that they will ignore. It is psychology, really, knowing what spreads well.'

Webmaster

Money: An experienced webmaster, with a good balance of technical and marketing skills, is hard to find, so can demand a good salary. The lowest you can expect will be around £20,000, but realistically you could expect £25,000 to £50,000, rising to £65,000 if you are known to be responsible for some hot marketing sites which draw plenty of customers and business.

Hours: In theory it will be classic marketing industry business hours of 10–6, but like most technical people you will probably be happy to work evenings and weekends too. It is possible to be a webmaster working from anywhere and at any time, although some face-to-face meetings in office hours will be necessary.

Health risk: Medium. Eyes, posture and joints can all suffer from prolonged computer use, but as this job involves lots of meetings too, you should be able to get plenty of breaks.

Pressure rating: Medium. Most webmasters like a bit of stress and having to work to deadlines. You'll have to ensure that sites are implemented and active on time, that all the links work and that the site is secure. And it must be updated regularly.

Glamour rating: Depends how you feel about working in IT – some think that anything connected with the Internet is glamorous, others that it's deadly dull, so it depends on your perspective, as well as the sites you are responsible for.

Travel rating: Low. There may be the occasional need to go to a client's premises to discuss their marketing strategy or to an IT show to see the latest products and services, but almost all your time will be spent at the computer screen or in local meetings within your company.

This is the person responsible for keeping the website of a marketing agency or consultancy and their clients updated on a day-to-day basis. Definitely a techie person, but also one familiar with marketing and on-line marketing concepts and strategies, because they are mainly responsible for content, not technology. It's a new science, a fairly new job and those who do it are constantly breaking new ground and making new rules.

Nicola Baker is a webmaster working in one of London's larger agencies. She studied IT and programming at university but says that her job in marketing is far more exciting than any others she considered. 'I love working in this sector. The people are so creative and fun, they have such wild ideas and I love working with them trying to make their schemes and campaigns a success.'

Nicola's time is split between working on websites, updating and fine-tuning existing sites and creating new ones, and playing with programming languages to develop new marketing techniques. She says, 'The Internet marketing manager and the new media team come to me with ideas and I try to put them into action.'

She also has to make sure that the marketing campaigns linked to clients' sites are working properly. She explains, 'You can't launch a new marketing campaign, invite the public to visit a client's site and then have the site keep crashing. So I have to know when the site is being advertised and marketed to make sure it delivers what everyone expects it to.'

She describes her job as being part creative design, part high technology and programming and part people management. 'It is computer based but I also have lots of meetings with brand and product managers and the marketing professionals, about what they'd like to see on the site. I have to translate what they want into good web practice.'

The problem with the Internet, says Nicola, is that customers are never more than a couple of clicks away from a competitor, so the trick is to try and keep them, to make the site sticky so that they will want to come back to it another time. 'I have to consider the overall site design, the page design and the interface with the user. All these have to be seen in the context of the image and brand that the product or company is trying to build, and its target market.

'The first thing I do is have a meeting with all the product and marketing people and establish their mission and objectives. We have to establish the immediate goals of the site and work out at the beginning how we will measure its success once it is up and running.'

Nicola has to remember that some users will be complete novices, so the site has to be easy for them to navigate, while others will be proficient surfers who should not be patronised. Also, some will be from overseas. 'It's not called the "World Wide Web" for nothing,' says Nicola. 'Readers could be people down the hall or in Australia. So we need to provide translations into other languages or use techniques and signs which are internationally understood.' This means that little things, such as the way that dates are arranged, have to be thought about carefully.

Internet technology also means that the webmaster can be located anywhere, and although Nicola prefers to work from an office, there is no reason why she shouldn't work from home or from an office in Scotland or Cornwall. 'Apart from meetings with clients and the marketing professionals,' she says, 'I could do the job from anywhere.

'Each member of the marketing team will have different goals and preferences and some will have web expertise, which can be a blessing or a curse,' she goes on. Unfortunately, web design teams rarely include members of the target audience, so she tries to hold meetings with the market research manager to get a good understanding of the target user.

Once Nicola has an idea of the website's marketing mission and the general structure that the marketing professionals have in mind, she begins to assess the content already available and to judge what needs to be created. 'Often the existing marketing material is inappropriate,' she says. 'Content for the web has to be more succinct, written more snappily and in a different style to paper based marketing material.'

Sometimes Nicola writes the new content herself, sometimes she liaises with the copywriters, who are becoming more skilful at web copy. 'I also have to develop a project plan and a budget,' she says. 'Content development can be the most time-consuming part of the job, so I often have to use third parties and other marketing professionals to get it right.'

Once the site is designed, Nicola is responsible for constructing it. Again, she sometimes uses a specialist web design house, just giving them the content and leaving it to them to choose the typeface and layout. 'The site also has to be marketed, but I leave that to the marketing professionals. It's my job to make sure the site works right and delivers the right marketing messages, but not to publicise it.'

Once the site is up, Nicola also has to track, evaluate and maintain it and, if possible, generate statistics on the number and type of people who have hit the site and logged on. 'Evaluation is tricky,' she says. 'But I have a methodology for giving a realistic return on investment.'

Getting a website working properly is a major part of any agency's or consultancy's own PR and marketing, and having the skills to manage their clients' sites, or at least the marketing aspects of them, is an important part of their portfolio.

Nicola says, 'Too many websites begin life as ad hoc efforts, created by small interest groups working in isolation from their peers or colleagues and without fully considering the site's goals within the context of the organisation's overall mission. The result is poorly planned, hasty development and an "orphan" site, starved of resources and attention.' She has to check and tweak about 15 sites a day, as well as working on new sites for clients.

Nicola says that site design involves finding out what the marketers and their clients like and how they like it, and making sure that the site gives that to them.'The site has an overall look and feel. The page design has to be as simple as possible, still getting all the necessary information across with clarity, order and accuracy,' she says. She recommends the job to anyone who loves working with the Internet, who has a technology bent and is also creative.'I don't have to think up the campaigns,' she says,'but I have to make sure they happen and the websites are kept up to date all the time.'

Nicola is currently investigating incorporating multimedia in her site designs.'We are about to have a shed-load more bandwidth available and will be able to include audio and video clips and have a far higher level of interactive contact with customers and surfers. This corner of marketing is terribly exciting – there are new things happening every day.'

Skills you'll need

- It's a toss-up whether the IT or graphic design skills are more important, but you certainly need a combination of both. You'll have to understand **HTML** and typography and understand the web as a marketing medium. Nicola says, 'I've had to learn programming on top of my graphic design background and I think that was the best approach for me. Maybe other people start with a technical background and are able to add the graphic design. There are specialist webmaster courses available to help develop and integrate the technical programming and design skills that are necessary. Most graphic design colleges these days offer a web design course.'

- You'll need good team and interpersonal skills. The webmaster may be in charge of what appears on a website (the content), how it works and where the hyperlinks are, but there will be plenty of contact with marketing professionals, other IT professionals and clients. So a combination of technical and interpersonal skills is critical. Nicola has frequent meetings with clients who have their own ideas as to what a site should offer.'I often have to explain that their ideas just wouldn't work,' she says.'There is a lot of expectation management and I have to be able to explain in their language what the technical and programming limits are.'

■ A good sense of style and design, the ability to be succinct in what you write and say and the ability to translate technical limitations and opportunities to non-technical marketing people and their clients.

■ You'll have to love programming and be adept at using the standard web design packages and languages. So the sooner you begin the better – start designing websites for friends, family and school or college, and try to accommodate everyone's wish list. Construct hot links to other people's e-mail addresses and websites and make the site as fast to load and easy to navigate as possible.

■ If you like spending 18 hours a day in front of the computer, start working on your people skills. The webmaster needs both IT and interpersonal talents. You can't have one without the other.

■ **HTML**
Hypertext mark-up language, a computer programming language used specifically for developing websites.

How to get into Marketing and PR

Appendix:

Professional bodies and courses

Professional bodies

- **British Market Research Association** (BMRA), 0800 801 785, www.bmra.org.uk
- **Chartered Institute of Marketing** (CIM), 0500 501 334
- **The Field Marketing Association** (FMA), 01628 789 689
- **Institute of Public Relations** (IPR), 020 7253 5151, info@ipr.org.uk
- Qualified advice to students during clearing: **www.careers-portal.co.uk**. Provides on-line advice on careers and tertiary education for careers in marketing and PR. Links to universities, recruitment agencies and career advisory services. 020 8486 1163, alexis@careers-portal.co.uk
- Study for Chartered Institute of Marketing (CIM) qualifications in your own time with a specialist Internet-based training organisation, **ftknowledge**. This provides CIM-approved study materials and case studies and uses the Internet to put students in contact with their tutor and other students. www.ftknowledge-cim.com
- **Cheltenham Tutorial College** offers CIM qualifications and a masters programme by distance learning. 01242 241 279, www.cheltenhamlearning.co.uk
- An Internet-based recruitment service on **www.erecruitment.com**, 020 7613 3323, does not advertise jobs but matches applicants with jobs and arranges interviews
- **Kingston University** has part-time marketing courses for those already in work. You can use your company as a guinea-pig for the marketing strategies taught by the tutors. Weekend or weekday attendance. 020 8547 7260, www.kingston.ac.uk
- **Manchester University** runs distance learning marketing courses with some residential weekends, to CIM diploma level. 0161 275 6361, www.mbs.ac.uk
- The **Open University Business School** runs marketing courses which are approved by the CIM. www.open.ac.uk
- **Surrey European Management School**, based at the University of Surrey, offers MSc programmes designed to

prepare students for a variety of specialist careers in management and marketing with full-time and part-time courses. Their programme includes an MSc in e-commerce. 0800 052 3976, 01483 259 237, www.sems.surrey.ac.uk

- **Thames Valley University** offers CIM qualifications in a variety of modules and courses, full- and part-time, and MBA qualifications. 020 8579 5000, www.tvu.ac.uk

Courses and qualifications

You are advised to gain professional training and qualifications in your chosen branch of marketing and PR. However, the quality, reputation and value of specific courses and qualifications are inclined to change over time, so you are advised to contact the professional body or bodies in your country to see which is currently recommended and also to talk to working professionals to see which they rate the most highly.

The International Public Relations Association currently has members in 92 countries including the USA, the European Community, South Africa, Europe, China and Australasia and many small nations too and is a good place to start for information about courses and qualifications: **www.ipranet.org**

Another place to find marketing and PR career information is **www.online-pr.com** where you will find international associations, details of PR and marketing magazines and newsletters and general resources for marketing and PR practitioners.

These sites may also be good starting points. Many have links to other sites:

www.adforum.com is an international portal to the professional communications world

www.admedia.org has links to internet marketing resources

www.ama.org is the American Marketing Association

www.corpcomstudies.com has a searchable database of more than 1,400 PR corporate communication companies

www.facsnet.org is a resource for journalists which marketeers should know about

www.geocities.com/Madison Avenue/1020 is a Swedish site which tracks PR and marketing globally

www.iabc.com is the International Association of Business Communicators

www.ipr.org.uk is the UK Institute of Public Relations

www.iprs.org.sg is the Institute of PR of Singapore

www.ire.rg is for investigative reporters and editors

www.marketing.org is the Business Marketing Association

www.martex.co.uk/prca is the Public Relations Consultants Association

www.mii.ie/ is the Irish Marketing Institute

www. mind-advertising.com is a directory of advertisers, agencies, brands and media in over 60 countries

www.naa.org is the Newspapers Association of America

www.naipra.org is the North American Association of Independent Public Relations Agencies

www.netpress.org is the Internet Press Guild for working on-line journalists

www.nsmi.com is the WWW marketing resource guide

www.prfirms.org is the council of public relations firms

www.prsa.rg is the Public Relations Society of America

www.responsesource. com is a resource for journalists

www.swisspr.cg is the Swiss Public Relations Institute

www.usprnet.com is a US national PR network

www.wepr.prg is for women executives in Public Relations

www.womcom.org is the Association for Women in Communications